Famou

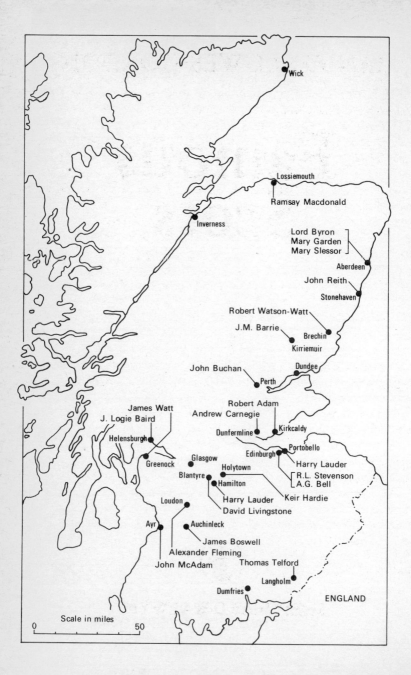

Wick

Lossiemouth
Ramsay Macdonald

Inverness

Lord Byron
Mary Garden
Mary Slessor

Aberdeen

John Reith

Stonehaven

Robert Watson-Watt

J.M. Barrie   Brechin
Kirriemuir

John Buchan   Dundee
          Perth

Robert Adam
Andrew Carnegie   Kirkcaldy
James Watt   Dunfermline
J. Logie Baird
Helensburgh   Portobello
          Edinburgh   Harry Lauder
Greenock   Glasgow   R.L. Stevenson
          Holytown   A.G. Bell
          Blantyre
Loudon   Hamilton
          Harry Lauder   Keir Hardie
Ayr   David Livingstone
          Auchinleck
          James Boswell
Alexander Fleming
John McAdam   Thomas Telford
          Langholm
          Dumfries
          ENGLAND

0   Scale in miles   50

IAN FELLOWES GORDON

Famous
Scots

SHEPHEARD·WALWYN

© IAN FELLOWES GORDON, 1988

ISBN 0 85683 105 0

Printed and bound in Great Britain
for Shepheard-Walwyn (Publishers) Ltd,
26 Charing Cross Road (Suite 34), London WC2H 0DH
by Cox & Wyman Ltd, Reading, Berkshire,
from typesetting by Alacrity Phototypesetters,
Banwell Castle, Weston-super-Mare.

Cover Design by Alan Downs

c.1

Contents

1/26/98 gift

Preface

The first book about Scotland was *The Life of Julius Agricola*, written by Tacitus, his dutiful son-in-law. It tells of the days in our first century A.D. when the Romans invaded North Britain. They hacked their way northward, and after two long years their large, well-trained, well-armed, army had got as far as the Firths of Forth and Clyde.

Not exactly a *blitzkrieg*. Indeed, from what Tacitus tells us of his father-in-law's campaign, it was painfully slow and horribly expensive in manpower. Much of Britain in those days was a forest broken up by squelching bog and sudden, unexpected, loch or stream. And it was always as the Roman army cursed its way through bog or stream that the North Britons descended and cut them to shreds.

So after two years of campaigning, Julius Agricola had made it only as far as the south banks of Clyde and Forth. And Tacitus points out, a trifle unkindly, that had he been fighting a unified people instead of a great many mutually quarrelsome tribes, he might never have got there at all.

But if Agricola thought his troubles were over, he was mistaken. The land of high hills beyond Forth and Clyde was inhabited by a tall and terrifying people with hair of a magic redness which to this day can be found only in Scotland. (There are red-headed descendants in plenty of those early Caledonians all over the world from Montreal to Malawi, but the startling hue has faded.) And these red-headed warriors from the mountains were not only the toughest nut Agricola had to crack — fierce, brave and immensely

1

strong — but they had the disconcerting habit of sweeping southward into the lands Agricola had already subdued and starting things up again. He hastily built a line of forts, right across the waist of the country, to stop them.

The Roman legions, and the forts, had a deterrent effect. Indeed, the Highlanders received a salutary lesson at the battle of what Tacitus calls *Mons Graupius*. The name has metamorphosed into "Grampian", and now those rugged hills are about all we have to remind us of the first recorded battle on Scottish ground.

But when Julius Agricola was recalled to Rome the Highlanders broke through his line of forts and entered the lands to the south.

This they have continued to do.

The strange, complex, amalgam of Pict and Scot and Briton and Saxon — and just plain Sassenach — has trickled, surged, and at times exploded over the Border ever since, civilizing the lesser breeds below — or perhaps just adding a little stiffening to a nation of shopkeepers. For although the Scotsmen of today number but a tenth of the United Kingdom population, they comprise more than a fifth of its professional people.

Indeed it has been said that the best thing for our twentieth-century world, and in particular for Scotland, would be for this exodus to speed up. If all these complex people could get away from their homeland and move outwards in some Celtic *Diaspora*, think what might happen: if Baird and Carnegie and Reith and Adam and Mary Garden had to get out to perform their wonders, think what five million more might do, sweeping across the globe. The mind boggles.

And then uncomplicated English shopkeepers, bucket-and-spade in hand, trousers rolled to the knee, fishing-rods at the ready, could move in and enjoy themselves — in the process commercializing the place to everyone's advantage, as a vast and splendid holiday camp.

But the Scots would never let them. For they are, as any English government from the time of Edward I can testify, a perverse people. They make, as everyone knows, the finest whisky in the world, and jealously guard the secret. They make a point of demanding so-and-so's brand of it in the pubs and shops and, unlike people in other climes who do the same, they know whether they get it or not.

But only in Scotland is it drunk with fizzy lemonade to drown the taste.

Not, of course, that even a sizeable minority would admit to the sacrilege.

Perhaps I just have the wrong friends. But I suppose I have, in Scotland, drunk as many gallons, sweet and fizzy, of our national drink, as in the generally accepted manner. We have loudly demanded so-and-so's brand — not always the same brand, but any of a number of rare and expensive ones found only in Scotland: and then, making sure that we have not been fooled or defrauded, we have mixed it reverently with fizzy lemonade from a screw-top bottle and gulped the lot.

And I have sat with a Scots copy-writer, dedicated to the proposition that cool, un-iced, spring water is the only permitted diluent of the national drink. And as he wrote his deathless prose he drank his Scotch by the tumbler. In pasteurized, homogenized, milk, with a lump of ice floating on top.

But all this is only a prelude — a warning, if you like — against what follows. You must judge for yourself, unless you already know, what the Scots are really like.

And — it must be added — the Scots herein are not *really* typical. They've been selected because a thread of eccentricity, a theme, unites them: these are the ones who left Scotland behind and achieved fame (or notoriety) beyond its borders.

This is certainly a Scots characteristic, but Dr Johnson's remark that a Scotsman's fairest prospect is the road leading south to England applies only to some. When I was a boy, there were old men who'd never in their lives travelled the 35 miles into Aberdeen. And were proud of it. There's a story of the old farmer who asked his minister, after kirk on the Sabbath, in what direction this 'Jerusalem' lay. A moment's orientation and the Rev. McTavish pointed east.

His parishioner beamed with delight. 'Och, I kennt fine it was a wee bit past Inverurie'.

Times have changed but many horizons are as limited.

For this is the Scottish paradox; many of us want to get out and tilt our lances at the world — and probably a higher percentage get out and do it, successfully, than from any other nation. But there is still a majority for whom Scotland *is* the world.

There has always been a strong emotional undertow dragging Scotland back to the past. Many of her inhabitants regard themselves as Scots, Scottish, Scotch (take your choice; there is no right or wrong) and not assimilated as 'British'. A vociferous minority would like their tenth of the UK population to have its own mini-Army, Navy and Air Force and a seat at the United Nations. I personally find this idea foolish and humiliating, and I react much as my late father (the most inwardly Scotch of Scots) would do on seeing a man wearing the kilt in a London street: cool contempt for an exhibitionist.

The Scots have contributed greatly to Britain (and, as this book hopes to point out) the rest of the world. But it would be nonsense to pretend they got nothing back, that they were not dependent, in a thousand different ways, on the other inhabitants of this island.

There is one Scottish obsession which I find quite pleasing. So many of us (though by no means all) want to head home at the end of the day. Like salmon from our Scottish rivers, we find our way back to the river which gave us life, and we struggle up it. To spawn (perhaps) and to die.

Here, set out with love and sometimes a little malice, are a score or so of the lives of men and women who shook Scotland's dust from their shoes and did their own thing. Not all were good, not all were clever, but I hope you may find their lives as fascinating as I have.

FAMOUS SCOTS

The Adam Brothers

South of the Strand in London are the dignified remains of a district made famous — indeed, *made* — by the Adam brothers. I suppose I had known the district, admired what survives of it, for years, and also been aware of the fact that it took its name from the brothers. I even pondered in my ignorance why they should have used only two letters of their honoured name in christening this child of stone.

It was some time later that my lack of the Greek was made good by the vital word. For Adelphi, as no doubt the reader could tell me, is not a pale derivative of 'Adam': it is the Greek word, *Adelphoi*, or 'brothers'.

It was by this that John, Robert, James and William wished to be remembered.

Sadly, a great deal of the Adelphi district, where men like George

Bernard Shaw, James Barrie and David Garrick lived, has been destroyed and replaced by glum, twentieth-century clusters of businessmen and typists. The streets, named after the individual brothers, are still there, though William Street has been renamed Durham House Street; some of the charm of this eighteenth-century Scottish confection still remains.

But as Garrick, who lived there, could testify, Scotsmen were not all that popular in mid-eighteenth-century England. Too many of them were coming south, taking the bread (and cake) from the mouths of Englishmen. Once, when they had been, if not popular, at least accepted, Garrick had produced a play by the Scots dramatist John Home. By 1769, when the same Home wrote his *The Fatal Discovery*, Scotsmen were so unpopular south of the border that Garrick, while purchasing the play, was forced to credit an Englishman with having written it.

The Fatal Discovery was an instant and overwhelming success. But as soon as the truth leaked out, the public stayed away in its thousands.

So although we must accept that the Adam brothers, and in particular Robert, were much admired in England for their work, we must add that the conditions under which they worked were not always ideal.

And yet this anti-Scottishness had not always been so. How many people know of the Scots architect — an Aberdonian, no less — who designed not only the lovely church of St. Mary's-le-Strand, but St. Martin-in-the-Fields, too? And a quantity of other graceful buildings which include the Radcliffe Library at Oxford. He lived a century before the Adams, James Gibbs.

Robert Adam was born on 3 July, 1728, in Kirkcaldy, the second surviving son of an eminently successful Scots architect, William Adam. Excepting those designed by his brilliant and prolific son, William Adam probably designed more of the large Scottish mansions we know than any other architect before or since.

John, the eldest of the four surviving into manhood, was born seven years before Robert, while James was born three years later. After that came William. There were also two sisters.

The four sons were encouraged to watch the father at his work, and probably the first any of them saw of this was the erection of Drum House at Gilmerton. By the time old William died, in 1748, he had designed a number of houses in Scotland, as well as the Edinburgh Orphans' Hospital and, in the same town, George Watson's Hospital and the Royal Infirmary. It was in this town that his son Robert, destined to be the most famous, got his education. He went to the High School, then the University.

The family was prosperous, and at the age of twenty-five he was sent to tour France and Italy. Already it had been decided he would be an architect like his father. He was a fine young man, tall and lean, with a strong jaw and a rugged, fighter's nose; and from what we can tell of all their portraits, of quite different appearance from his brothers.

His travels about the Continent have been little documented, though for years people believed he had published a journal — until it was proved that it related to travels, years later, of his brother James. There are fine drawings and plans he made in Italy, including the impressive 'Design for a Royal Palace' done at Rome in 1757.

Among the things Robert Adam studied in Italy were ruins at Spalato, and he completed the drawing of these in record time. For as he wrote later, the Venetian governor, 'unaccustomed to such visits of curiosity from strangers, began to conceive unfavourable sentiments of my intentions, and to suspect that under pretence of taking views and plans of the Palace, I was really employed in surveying the state of the fortifications". He was stopped, then managed to get grudging permission to carry on. 'The fear of a second interruption added to my industry, and by unwearied application during five weeks, we completed, with an accuracy that afforded me great satisfaction, those parts of our work which it was necessary to execute on the spot.'

(He later published a book on the subject, with these plans and sketches in it, and England was greatly impressed. But by that time he was already a success.)

On his return from Italy in 1758 he settled in London, in the Lower Grosvenor Street house where he lived until his Adelphi was built, years later.

Almost immediately he became famed as a scholarly architect of great ability. And one can perhaps see reason for some of the anti-Scottish sentiment that arose because Scots were skimming the cream off England, when we read that Adam was invited by Lord Coventry to vet the work being done on his Croome Court by Lancelot, 'Capability', Brown (who was both architect and garden designer); Lord Scarsdale asked his opinion on Kedleston which was being built; the future Lord Harewood invited his views on the embryo Harewood House near Leeds. We can only guess at what architects Brown, Brettingham, Paine and Carr thought about this.

But his first actual work in England was the designing of furiture and appointments for houses — which included all those mentioned above. He felt strongly that each piece of furniture, each carpet, each fitting, must be designed in accordance with the general scheme of the house. To prove his point, he started designing cabinets, carpets, tapestries, mirrors, fanlights, fireplaces, doors, himself.

His designs were furiously copied by others, so that today it is difficult to say who made a chair in 'The Adam Style'. And, in fact, many of these were made, but with permission and encouragement from his elder brother, by James Adam.

In 1773, after Robert had been practising in England for fifteen years, the first part of the *Works of Robert and James Adam* was published. In it the brothers stated, 'Our ambition is to share with others, not to appropriate to ourselves, the applause of the public, and if we have had any claim to approbation, we found it on this alone: that if we flatter ourselves we have been able to seize, with some degree of success, the beautiful spirit of antiquity and to transfuse it with novelty and variety through all our works.'

From interior design, the Adam brothers had gone on to plan houses. By an apparently amicable arrangement they found themselves completing Kedleston, in Derbyshire, which Paine had begun. Paine seems to have acquiesced cheerfully, owing to other work, in having the owner put 'this great work in the hands of those able and ingenious artists, Messrs. Robert and James Adam—'

But while the structural work was being done, Robert Adam had much else to deal with, including the stately Shardeloes in Buckinghamshire; erecting a screen to hide the unimaginative shape of the

Admiralty in London; and designing ceilings, chimney-pieces, doorways and furniture all over England.

Young James had gone on his own continental tour in 1760. Thanks to his journal, we have an interesting record of his travels and his impressions, from which we can conjecture what his older brother had done and thought.

Boodle's Club, an interesting example in London of Adam's work, was built in about 1765. While it went up, the brothers did work at Fonthill in Wiltshire and Witham House in Somerset. They also began taking on work in Ireland.

Prosaically — but prosaic in name only — Robert was appointed Clerk of the Works at the Royal Chelsea Hospital. His job was to keep all the buildings in repair and prepare estimates for the work, but he has left behind a legacy of beauty: if you were Robert Adam, your repairs involved rather more than replacing the odd slate and pointing up the brickwork.

By this time he had begun one of his masterpieces, *replacing* the interior (not just decorating it) of Syon House, home of the Duke of Northumberland. (And with the perversity that characterizes English dukes it had been built hundreds of miles from Northumberland, near London: His Grace of Marlborough, as we all know, had elected to put his own 'Blenheim' in Oxfordshire.) Syon is today one of the great show-places of England, about which Adam himself wrote:

> I endeavoured to render it a noble and elegant habitation, not unworthy of a proprietor who possessed not only wealth to execute a design but skill to judge of its merit. Some inequality of the old walls, and some want of additional heights to the enlarged apartments were the chief difficulties with which I had to struggle. These difficulties, I flatter myself, are in a great measure surmounted so as not only to procure such convenience in the arrangements of the apartments, but likewise an elegant form and graceful proportion in the principal rooms. The inequality of levels has been managed in such a manner as to increase the scenery and add to the movement, so that an apparent defect has been converted into a real beauty.

Obviously the best way to enjoy the work of an architect or a designer is to see it. Here we must content ourselves with the man alone, and fortunately a lot of him is in the written word. He was a man of many parts, destined even to be a Member of Parliament (but only, as was the pleasing custom, in his spare time). As he wrote in the Adam brothers 'Works', it was important to have been to France to study the customs 'of that social and conversible people'. But, he went on, 'in one particular our manners prevent us from imitating them. Their eating rooms seldom or never constitute a piece of their great apartments, but lie out of the suite; and in fitting them up little attention is paid to beauty of decoration. The reason of this is obvious: the French meet there only at meals, when they trust to the display of the table for show and magnificence; and as soon as the entertainment is over, they immediately retire to the rooms of the company. It is not so with us. Accustomed by habit, or induced by the nature of our climate, we indulge more largely in the enjoyment of the bottle. The eating rooms are considered as the apartments of conversation, in which we are to pass a great part of our time.'

And so the eating rooms at Syon are ornate — and beautiful.

So, too, is the rest. One of the more remarkable bits is the so-called Vestibule, the room at the south-west corner, with its ten green marble columns enclosing a central space about twenty-five feet square. The capitals and bases of the columns are gilded and carved. The shafts themselves are of a marble dredged up from the bed of the River Tiber, and they cost the duke a cool £1,000 each — way back in the eighteenth century.

And, of course, with this extensive interior re-building there had to be the designing of furniture and fitments to go with it.

The list of houses which Robert and James re-modelled and extended — and on occasion built — is enormous. One that still stands monument to their skill and taste is Kenwood in Hampstead. Others, to name only a few, are Bowood in Wiltshire, Harewood House in Yorkshire, Luton Hoo in Bedfordshire.

And while all this was going on, the eldest brother, John, was working as an architect in Scotland. In 1767 he began Jamaica Street Bridge over the Clyde at Glasgow — and in the following year Robert himself, not forgetting his origins, was elected Member of Parliament for Kinross. In those days Kinross and Clackmannan elected a representative in turn, and Robert served until the next election when it was time for a Member to be returned from Clackmannan. After this he seems cheerfully to have given up this political sideline.

But it was at the time he took his seat that all four brothers got together to lease Durham Yard in London, off the Strand, and build their 'Adelphi' on it. The yard was a hideous neighbourhood of hovels, mean streets and bad smells, sloping sharply to the river, where the stink was even worse. The brothers hit upon an ingenious but expensive plan: to avoid having to build on a slope, and to get dwellings away from the foul-smelling water, they would raise the whole of their new residential area far above the river by constructing a series of vaults in brickwork. This would be much like making a flat raft of their building land, supported on immense barrels.

They were led to believe the government would lease these vaults from them as store houses — and this, they rashly assumed, would defray some of the cost.

In another move to keep down cost, they imported their labourers from Scotland, where wages were lower. A splendidly immoral plan, which has been adopted more than once in this century.

But the Adams had their troubles. When their Scots workmen found out what Englishmen were being paid, they immediately went on strike. At this point, so history relates, the brothers got hold of Irishmen and completed the work.

When the thing had been built, the four brothers then introduced a Bill into Parliament seeking to reclaim more land from the Thames by erecting at their own cost an embankment. Their good friend and fellow-architect, James Paine, with whom they had once competed, joined them in the petition. Against much opposition from the City of London, the Bill was passed, in 1771.

Seldom has so ambitious a scheme been embarked on by private enterprise. Had it not been so costly, the actual buildings would have been grander, more expansive, but by the time the vaults had been laid on the river bank, there was a decided shortage of money for completing the scheme. All manner of buildings had been planned, and not all were built. Among those that *were* built were the Adelphi Chapel and the School of Arts. In April, 1772, Robert Adam himself moved into one of the many private houses, one in the street that still bears his Christian name, while the names of the other three brothers were given to other streets on the site. Among the first to move in was their friend David Garrick, and as the area immediately became highly desirable, the actor was besieged by men and tradesmen who wanted to get there, too. Becket the bookseller asked him to intercede with the four Scotsmen, and Garrick wrote them:

> My dear Adelphi, I forgot to speak to you last Saturday about our friend Becket. We shall all break our hearts if he is not bookseller at the Adelphi and has not the corner house that is to be built. Pray, my dear and very good friends, think a little of this matter, and if you can make us happy by suiting all our conveniences, we shall make his shop, as old Jacob Tonson's was formerly, the rendezvous for the first people in England.

Becket got his shop. But there was trouble ahead. The government welshed on its agreement to use the vaults as storehouses, and soon the brothers were in very serious financial trouble. Yet Parliament — perhaps through the good offices of the Member for Kinross — seems to have been on their side. They were saved by a Lottery Bill, passed in 1773, which gave permission for them to dispose of their buildings by means of a lottery. The idea is not as bizarre as it seems, for in the eighteenth century Parliament often permitted lotteries to be held 'for desirable purposes'. One of these, twenty years earlier, had been for the establishment of the first British Museum.

The lottery for the Adelphi buildings netted a sizeable profit and the brothers were solvent again.

Their fame grew, and the Adelphi, though it had taken on some of the notoriety of a South Sea Bubble, remained a monument to the four Adam brothers for a hundred and fifty years, till much of it was pulled down in the 1930s. While they lived, the brothers went on building or decorating houses all over London and all over Britain.

Robert Adam died in 1792 at the age of sixty-three, in London. He was still unmarried, and he left his effects to his two sisters, Elizabeth and Margaret. John, the eldest, died in the same year, in Edinburgh. James followed them into the grave two years later, and William, the youngest, was left with the job of supervising all the work they had begun and left unfinished. He did this in the intervals of erecting buildings to his own design, right up to the time of his death at Edinburgh in 1822.

Quite a family. What did they achieve?

They were clannish and devoted, on the Scots pattern. Had they been English we would have heard only of Robert, for he was really the great architect of the team, and the others, though he encouraged them in their work, were basically little more than business associates. We must make up our own minds whether Robert was a genius or not. After Kedleston and Syon, we can look at Osterley; Kenwood; Harewood; at what survives of the Adelphi, and at Fitzroy Square. And farther north, at work he did towards the end of his life, at Charlotte Square in Edinburgh, and at the University.

There is a theory that all painting, architecture, of this period held the seeds of decay; that with Britain about to plunge into the horrors of an Industrial Revolution, some divine or satanic hand made architecture, in these last years of the eighteenth century, more elegant, less real. Sacheverell Sitwell, writing of eighteenth-century architecture, comes out with the theory, 'Adam created so easily that difficulty must be coming. And, indeed, in a few more years, architecture was dead completely.'

We may argue. But if architecture really died in that last decade of the eighteenth century, it had a lovely funeral.

James Boswell

When first I planned this book, I'd a brief confusion over dates. I have the dubious knack of linking events with each other, by the day or year in which they happened. Usually the events are as unrelated as the proverbial chalk and cheese, but they clutter up my brain like ill-matched couples in some undersized ballroom. Charles Wesley was born in the year of union between England and Scotland (though not as a result of that coupling). My house dates from the year Shakespeare was born. My labrador bitch was born on the anniversary of Pearl Harbour. And so on and so on — each link more puzzling and unhelpful than the one before.

Sometimes I get them wrong. Which is why I had James Boswell set firmly in 1714, the year of George I's accession. Not in his rightful slot — 1740.

This would have been tiresome. I really couldn't start off with a snob, a drunk and a womaniser whose powers of selection were so poor that he spent sizeable chunks of his time undergoing painful treatment for ailments 'with which Venus sometimes plagues her votaries'. But chronologically he seemed to come first, and in a book of this sort one can only assemble one's team in that order. One can't begin with 'most important', and work on down, because we have no yardstick.

Fortunately, I discovered my mistake and was able to start with the Adam Brothers — a far more respectable introduction.

And having done so, I can slide gently on, a dozen years, to the life of that engaging buffoon and genius, James Boswell, who was born 29 October, 1740, in Edinburgh.

Almost from that day, Boswell had extravagant plans for becoming an officer in the Guards (London ceremonial duties only); a Member of Parliament; a nobleman and 'a fully rounded man of character.'

He never achieved any of these goals. But I think one of the several pleasant things one can say about Boswell as a man is that the determination to become a fully-rounded man of character was the ambition uppermost in his mind, to the day he died. He was 55, and convinced that he'd been a failure.

He wasn't, of course, and he left behind him a far bigger reputation than most men.

To some, though, he remains the little man with a notebook pursuing a scrofulous, ill-mannered Dr. Johnson, jotting down the pundit's every word. A reporter, grasping the chance to gain fame by immortalising a grumpy old man who, without Boswell's biography of him, would have left little impress on history. Johnson was a brilliant man, but so were others of his circle, and few would quarrel with the verdict that he talked far, far better than he wrote. His crowning achievement was that least readable of literary efforts, a dictionary. To give the man his due (which was more than his rapacious publishers did) the commissioned 'Dictionary of the English Language' was generally agreed to be the first dictionary that *could* be read for pleasure. The definitions showed 'great acuity of thought and command of language' and the passages quoted from poets and philosophers were so well selected 'that a leisure hour may be agreeably spent turning over the pages.'

In one respect, his dictionary was a failure. He knew almost nothing of etymology, even in the Latin and Greek he wrote so well. As a result, his derivations were usually nonsensical inventions. This in itself would hardly matter if Johnson hadn't tried to justify his invention by altering the meaning of the word, as in 'internecine'. It meant simply 'fought to the death', from the Latin *internecare*, to exterminate, and there was nothing 'mutual' in this Latin use of *inter*, any more than there is in *interire*, to perish. But Johnson assumed there must be and gave us the completely new meaning of 'endeavouring mutual destruction'. As this is now used by the word-happy to signify a verbal argument within, say, the Labour Party and not a shoot-out on the front benches, the meaning has changed beyond all recognition. Lexicographers have carefully copied Johnson's mistake, though the Oxford Concise does note 'Orig: deadly'.

In any case, a dictionary, however long its gestation, can only be ephemeral. Pronunciation, meaning, spelling, subtly metamorphose, while new words are coined and old ones drop by the wayside.

Having said this, one must add that Dr Samuel Johnson was a genius, dogged by so much personal misfortune — grinding poverty, permanent ill-health, an unfortunate marriage — that he hardly had the opportunity to realise his extraordinary potential. So, as he left so little of value behind him, we must get the facts from the voluminous writings of the man who styled himself 'James Boswell, Esquire, proud Scot of ancient lineage'; and occasionally (quite without justification) 'Baron Boswell'.

The study of Boswell continues and we must be deeply indebted to Yale University, above all others, for revealing the man in a sympathetic light and then continuing over the years to collate the mountains of Boswell's writing. These have appeared in cupboards, in boxes of sports equipment, and as the wrappings of parcels. They've been turning up ever since Boswell's death in 1795 and one can only guess at what the next lot may appear as.

The writings prove James Boswell to be far from just a cub reporter. Boswell was a man in search of himself, and the 'lion-hunting' was an attempt to learn, to educate himself, through great and wise men.

Never can man have analysed himself so closely, day after day. 'I think too closely. I am too concave a being. My thoughts go inwards too much instead of being carried out to external objects. I wish I had a more convex mind.' Not only did he scribble down these reflections just before going to bed, or on rising, but he drew up (and constantly revised) his own private 'Scheme Of Living'. Writing on his second arrival in London, 1762, he notes: 'My allowance from my father is £25 every six weeks; in all, £200 a year. To support the rank of a gentleman with this is difficult. Yet I hope to do it in the following manner:'

There follows a break-down of planned expenditure — a budget — which leaves him annually just £43, 'for coach hire, diversion, and the tavern, which I will find a very slight allowance ... If I get a commission in the Guards, I shall then have about £90 a year more, which will make me pretty easy.'

We have shown him as Worried Introvert, and Cautious Planner; let us just glance at Boastful Boswell: 'Surely I am a man of genius. I deserve to be taken notice of. O that my grandchildren might read this character of me: "James Boswell, a most amiable man. He improved and beautified his paternal estate of Auchinleck; made a distinguished figure in Parliament; had the honour to command a regiment of footguards, and was one of the brightest wits in the court of George the Third."'

James never made the Guards (and he refused a commission in a marching regiment because it lacked glamour). He never made Parliament, and he was never much involved, witty or not, with the court of George III. He was a perfectly adequate custodian of Auchinleck's acres after the death of his father (and in 1986 the Scottish Historic Buildings Trust bought the house, "once the home of Dr Johnson's biographer", to turn it into a centre for 18th-century Scottish studies).

One cannot resist a further quote, because it reveals still more. "What a curious, inconsistent thing is the mind of man! In the midst of divine service I was laying plans for having women, and yet I had the most sincere feelings of religion."

Most of Boswell's womanising was not through "laying plans", but on impulse and after drinking. One day in London he got drunk and "in a kind of brutal fever, went to the Park and was relieved by dalliance." This was his euphemism for sex — and when Boswell finds it in the Park, he has it then and there, standing up or lying down. Continuing this same evening, he has a further bottle of claret and more dalliance with another girl. And finally, on his way to his lodgings, he is 'picked up by a strumpet at the head of St James's Street', and has her too.

This might be considered enough for one man, but after a few hours' rest, and with a monumental hangover, Boswell goes out again, picking up girls in the Park. And — when one of these 'moods' affects him, the same thing goes on, day after day, until he takes a grip on himself and forswears both women and wine.

Though not for long. And sometimes this abstinence is brought on when he feels 'an alarm of unexpected evil: a little heat in the members of my body sacred to Cupid....'

But to start at the beginning: He was born 29 October 1740, in Edinburgh, where his father, Alexander Boswell, laird of the Ayrshire estate of Auchinleck, had a second residence from which he conducted his profession of Advocate. He'd reached a great height in that calling, as Lord of Session in Scotland's High Court, and as result, was a leader of Edinburgh society. The Scots had retained their own legal system after the Union of 1707 (and still do), so it was a symbol of Scottish nationhood. The infant Boswell was born with at least a silver-plated spoon in his mouth.

At the age of 6, he is attending James Mundell's excellent school in the city: a couple of years later, being taught by private tutors — apparently because of a nervous disposition. But by the age of 13 he is able to attend Edinburgh University (quite a normal age for the period) where he seems to have dabbled in just about everything from Roman antiquities to Botany before settling down, at his father's insistence, to the Law.

In fact, the teenage Boswell had been swept up in the exciting theatrical life of Scotland's capital city, and was delightedly consorting with actors and actresses, while scribbling verses for the

Scots Magazine, as well as his own reviews of the Edinburgh theatre.

His father got to hear of this and swiftly transferred young James to the far duller University of Glasgow. The move confused and enraged the boy, who in rapid succession became a Methodist, a Freemason, and — very nearly — a Roman Catholic. His letter to his staunchly Presbyterian father in February 1760, announcing the decision to become a priest, resulted in an angry summons to return home immediately.

Boswell simply rode away, on horseback, to London.

What did he look like, this 19-year-old runaway?

It seems he was strong and robust, of average height (5 feet six inches then) and plump. He had a rather swarthy complexion with very black hair and eyes. He was addicted to fine clothes and scrupulous about 'clean linen' but even this failed to make him a particularly handsome or impressive figure. He was (much of the time) aware of his shortcomings, but his reaction on first sighting London was one of unbridled delight.

From now on, though he would spend much time in Scotland, he was an Englishman by adoption. His plans for becoming a priest were swiftly replaced by one for losing his virginity and he seems to have had no trouble. Sally Forrester initiated him into 'the melting and transporting rites of love' in the Blue Periwig tavern off the Strand — and he never looked back.

But Boswell's father (who as a judge was entitled to the honorific 'Lord Auchinleck') was no fool. He decided the only way to deal with his headstrong, moody son was to introduce him to a fellow Ayrshireman, Lord Eglinton, who lived in London, was fond of its pleasures and familiar with them all while being an intimate of the greatest in the land. Eglinton took the lad under his wing, showed him the wonders of London and deeply impressed him.

Boswell decided to abandon all thoughts of a legal career. With what seems amazing impertinence he wrote his father — who'd set his heart on that career — asking for money to buy himself a commission in a Guards regiment. And Lord Auchinleck actually came down to London to see if, by a combination of money and his own influence with the Duke of Argyll, he could get one for his son and make him happy.

But things were moving so slowly that Auchinleck was able to persuade Boswell to come home to Scotland and think things over. And so, after a scant four months in London, he was back in the Edinburgh house where his family always spent much of the year.

Sullenly, he refused an offer of a commission in a marching regiment. Very well — if there was no immediate likelihood of getting one in the Guards, James Boswell would return to his Law books. But reluctantly.

He passed his exam in Civil Law in July 1762, at the age of 21. Then, to his surprise, Lord Auchinleck gave his blessing to a second, longer, stay in London. It seems an active career in Law was of comparatively little importance, set against the distinction and honour of simply being a lawyer.

His legal qualifications were of no use in England, so Boswell's only means of augmenting the allowance his father now offered was through his writings which at this early stage were puny, derivative and earned little praise or money. The young man could have another try, on his own, at a commission in the Guards and if, as Auchinleck forecast, he failed, no doubt he would return and continue his legal studies, ultimately passing as 'Advocate'.

Whatever the long term future might hold, James Boswell was 'a free man' and overjoyed. He was only a few days past his 22nd birthday, and he'd made so many influential friends during his earlier truancy that he had no doubt of his ability to live in modest style for as long as he liked.

But an important thing happened on his way south. Boswell agreed to join his new friend and father-figure, Lord Kames, in a tour of the Border countries, where the Kames estates were, before actually crossing into England. And the result was the first of the remarkable journals he was to keep throughout his life: 'Journal Of My Harvest Jaunt, 1762'.

He had no intention of getting this published: it was for the eyes of a few friends only. Which is a pity, though we can read and enjoy it today, thanks to Yale University. Had it been discovered by a publisher, Boswell's career might have been established from that moment. No man has ever conveyed a situation, a character, a scene in such fascinating detail. No man has ever selected so perfectly the anecdote that reveals the character of the person described (and at the same time, the character of James Boswell). He was, though it would be years before the English-speaking world discovered it, the finest biographer, ever, in that language.

Boswell's second stay in the metropolis, though longer than his first, was for only eight and a half months, and yet his 'London Journal, 1762-63' is a fat volume which sets out in vivid detail so many experiences, personalities, ideas and moods that one finds it hard to realise it all happened to one man in so short a time.

But Boswell's life during those months between November 1762 and August 1763 was much like the lives of many other young men in London. The difference lies in the telling — the extraordinary insight, the memory which locks on to every telling phrase of a conversation, each detail of dress or mannerism. This too was never published in his lifetime, because it was written in instalments, sometimes immediately after a certain event, sometimes a while later, and sent off to a friend in Scotland. His feelings for Scotland were certainly ambiguous. He remained proud of his nationality at a time when the Scots were highly unpopular in London. At a theatre when the audience, just before the play, started shouting abuse at two Highland officers among them, Boswell leapt up on his bench and swore long and vehemently at the demonstrators.

At the theatre, which he patronised often, and where, as there were no 'booked seats', one arrived early and entertained oneself before the play began, he liked to draw attention to himself. Apart from getting up and making impromptu and sometimes violent speeches on any subject which entered his head, he might entertain the audience by imitating farmyard noises. His impersonation of a cow was particularly well regarded.

At the same time, he was continually ashamed of the Scottish way in which he spoke, and was trying to rid himself of the accent and speech forms of his native tongue.

Which brings us conveniently to 16 May 1763, the most important day in Boswell's life. It was then, after he'd been drinking tea in the back room of a bookshop in Russell Street, that the great Dr

Samuel Johnson came in. And what were Boswell's first words on being introduced? 'Indeed, I come from Scotland, but I cannot help it.'

Boswell faithfully recorded this asinine remark, and Johnson's crushing reply. One might assume their relationship to have ended before it began, but Boswell persevered in trying to win the older man's friendship. A week after their first meeting, he boldly called on Johnson at his chambers in the Inner Temple, and was treated cordially. 'Upon my word,' he scribbed in his Journal that night, 'I am very fortunate. I shall cultivate this acquaintance.'

And so he did, with great success, though without any intention at the time of writing a Life of Dr Johnson, simply for the wisdom he hoped to acquire from regular contact with a man so wise. And of course, the other valuable contacts, like Burke, Reynolds, Garrick, Goldsmith and many others he expected to pick up in the great man's wake.

On 25 June he spent an evening with Johnson at the Mitre Tavern, and, in that curious mixture of boastfulness and humility which always characterised Boswell, he poured out his life story. Johnson was touched by it, and cried out, 'Give me your hand. I have taken a liking to you.' They were friends at last.

So great was this friendship that when Boswell set off on a visit to the Continent — a special bribe from his father before returning to Scotland and his studies — Johnson travelled with him by stage-coach to the port of Harwich, dined with him there and waved a farewell as the packet boat sailed for Holland.

We have no space to chronicle Boswell's adventures in Holland, Germany, Italy and Corsica, which lasted from August 1763 to March 1766. Ever on the lookout for famous, and wise, friends, he attached himself to Rousseau (whose mistress he seduced), Voltaire and the Corsican patriot leader Paoli, with whom he maintained contact until their deaths. On his return to London he sought out Dr Johnson and picked up the threads of their friendship as if he'd never been away.

Boswell's European tour was, of course, a great deal longer than his father intended, and the old gentleman was considerably dis-pleased — particularly as Lady Auchinleck had died two months before he saw fit to return. (On learning the news, Boswell consoled himself with a visit to a Paris brothel.) But now, back on British soil, he could make no more excuses. His 1766 stay in London was a very brief one.

Back in Scotland, chastened by the loss of his mother, but buoyed up by the wealth of experience he felt he'd gained on the Continent, he buckled down to his studies and was formally admitted as a Scots Advocate on 29 July 1766, at the age of 25.

For the next few years he was nominally a practising Scottish lawyer, but managed to spend a remarkable amount of time in London. As he'd long since abandoned hopes of a career in the Guards, his ambitions were to be a rich and successful author and a Member of Parliament. Success was to come in the former, but, sadly, very late in life; and his hopes of becoming an M.P. were doomed. He wasted great chunks of life in pursuit of that foolish ambition, yet however much he might delude himself that this or that influential person had, like Johnson, 'taken a liking' to him and would help him towards a political career, not a soul believed him capable of doing the job: he would disgrace his Party by getting drunk and delivering ludicrous, endless speeches.

It seems a fair prognosis. To the end of his life he lacked self-confidence and anything approaching a clear judgment: he depended on others.

And yet, for that abiding interest in others, the world must be deeply grateful. As biographer and diarist, he was, and remains, in a class of his own.

In 1769 he married his first cousin, Margaret Montgomerie. It had begun with the unconfident Boswell seeking her advice about love affairs he believed he'd started. Eventually he decided that though she was two years his senior and not beautiful, he'd stop asking questions and marry her. She agreed.

Margaret was a wise, understanding and unbelievably tolerant wife. Her sex drive was less than his, so it was only weeks before he was in the arms of a whore. Then another, and another.

And yet, strange man, he always told her and begged her forgiveness. She gave it — with diminishing eagerness over the years.

He was delighted when, in 1773, during one of his visits to

London, he was approached by Dr Johnson with a plan that they visit the highlands and islands of Scotland. Johnson had always wondered how 'this brave aboriginal people' behaved in their native habitat, and he would like a congenial guide.

They went, of course. And Boswell's 'Journey Of A Tour To The Hebrides With Samuel Johnson', written a year after Johnson's death, is vivid, colourful and totally fascinating. Johnson's own account is pedantic, pompous and dull.

And so life moves on, with Boswell, bored in Edinburgh but earning reasonable money as a part-time Advocate, writing more and more for periodicals and publishing more and more pamphlets on every subject under the sun. And having longer and longer stays in London.

Boswell was in London from 5 May 1784. Johnson had been quite seriously ill, but now seemed 'greatly recovered'. He saw a lot of the older man during the next few weeks, including dinner with him on 22 June after having, of his own volition, 'been present at the shocking sight of fifteen men executed before Newgate' (always a macabre obsession of Boswell's).

On 30 June Boswell and Johnson both dined at Sir Joshua Reynolds' house, and it was in the carriage afterwards that they had their last conversation, and 'bade adieu to each other'. When Johnson reached his house and got down on the pavement, 'he called out "Fare you well" and without looking back sprung away with a kind of pathetic briskness, if I may use that expression, which seemed to indicate a struggle to conceal uneasiness, and impressed me with a foreboding of our long, long separation.'

A little later, Johnson was dead, and Boswell heart-broken. He'd already decided to write the great man's life and now he became obsessed with collecting memorabilia, writings, anecdotes from every source.

Two years later, in 1786, he moved permanently to London and his wife was much upset. His father had died, he himself was now laird of Auchinleck, but she and the children must stay there, while he worked on his Life Of Johnson — and kept on hoping for a seat in Parliament.

Several times he thought he was nearing that goal, but found he wasn't, and he took to gambling, drinking and whoring even more furiously. His health suffered, but the blameless, almost saintly Mrs Boswell died of TB in June 1789. Overcome with shame and guilt, he brought four of his five children down to Great Portland Street in London. (One remained at an Edinburgh boarding school.)

His great biography appeared two years later, in 1791. But though it was a huge success, he regarded himself as a failure: not an M.P., not a Guards officer, not a wit at the King's Court.

He died, 19 May 1795, after a short illness — not knowing that he'd already achieved a fame far greater than all this.

James Watt

"It was in the Green of Glasgow, I had gone to take a walk on a fine Sabbath afternoon. I had entered the Green by the gate at the foot of Charlotte Street — had passed to the old washing-house. I was thinking upon the engine at the time, and gone so far as the Herd's house when the idea came into my mind that, as steam is an elastic body, it would rush into a vacuum, and if communication were made between the cylinder and an exhausted vessel, it would rush into it, and might there be condensed without cooling the cylinder —'

And so great ideas are born, as men wander and ponder, taking their walks on a fine Sabbath afternoon. The idea that now occurred to the instrument-maker James Watt was to change the shape of the world. Had James Watt never lived, someone else would have invented a practical steam engine — years later. Destiny produced this quiet, simple man just at the moment when his engine and all that followed from it would put Britain at the head of the world. For the coming of Watt's engine was a mechanical revolution which in turn spawned the Industrial Revolution, in which Britain — not entirely to her credit — would lead the world. The pace would be tremendous: the huge increase in manufacturing occasioned by this noisy, gasping monster of an engine would disorganize, dislocate factory managements and all the economic systems of the western world — particularly Britain's. Men and women would flock into overcrowded towns to work in factories and bring about an overcrowding and concentration of misery with which we are still struggling.

The fault would not be James Watt's: the misery attendant on his monster would be the result of other people's greed, the greed of factory owners and of peasants, of rich men and poor.

Watt would see little of this, for he died in 1819. Five years after that, a statue of him was placed in Westminster Abbey, and perhaps the inscription on its base puts more succinctly, and at least as accurately as I can, the real achievement of

'JAMES WATT
Who, directing the forces of an original genius,
Early exercised in philosophic research
to the improvement of
THE STEAM ENGINE,
enlarged the resources of his country,
increased the power of men,
and rose to an eminent place among the most
illustrious followers of science and the real
benefactors of the world.'

He was born in Greenock on the Clyde, in 1736, and there is a famous — and probably absurd — engraving of him by J. W. Steel, sitting as a small boy in that house in Greenock, watching in wonder, chin in hands, as the steam rises from a kettle on the stove. His mother is at the back of the room, chattering: she hasn't noticed the lid of the kettle being prised off by steam. Only the cat and James are watching, with clouds of the white vapour swirling about them.

The picture could really have been painted of dozens of other small boys. Robert Boyle, Edward Somerset, Christiaan Huygens, Thomas Savery, Denis Papin, Thomas Newcomen — and many others — could have been drawn in the same wondering attitude, all of them fascinated by the properties of this 'steam' (though it wasn't) coming from the boiling water. All of these, and others, experimented with it: it was left to James Watt to produce a satisfactory 'steam engine'.

He was the fourth of five children of a skilled carpenter who went on from the building of houses and ships to be a general merchant and a town councillor of Greenock. The young James Watt was a sickly child, too weak to go to school at the right age; and when he did go he was a poor specimen who did badly at his studies and was bullied by everyone.

He was no good at studies — but his father had the insight to realize the boy could become an engineer, for he showed an interest and a natural aptitude. He was given a workshop, all his own, in the attic, and there he made working models of barrel-organs, pumps, pulleys, a crane.

His mother's death coinciding with the family's sudden financial difficulty made him realize he must give up any thought of the university: he must go out now and earn his living.

How did a boy who made toy barrel-organs set about making a living?

He would be an instrument-maker. But first he would have to find one to teach him his trade: he moved to London.

At first, London seemed unpromising. As he wrote his father, he had been to visit a number of instrument-makers with a Glasgow professor's letter of introduction, but 'I have not yet got a Master, they all make some objection or other'.

At last he found one, who was a businessman as well as an instrument-maker, for he demanded a fee of twenty guineas. Having handed this over, James could work with him — and without pay — for twelve months.

He agreed, and the bargain — though his father was hard put to it sending down sufficient money to keep the lad — was a success. Mr. Morgan seems to have been one of the very few men in London able to teach all the things Watt felt he must know: 'Though he works chiefly in the brass way, yet he can teach me most branches of the business, such as rules, scales, quadrants, etc.' And by the end of his training, in 1757, aged twenty-one, he was able to write, modestly, 'I think I shall be able to get my bread anywhere as I am now able to work as well as most journeymen, though I am not so quick as many'.

A brief visit with his father in Greenock, and then to Glasgow. He went to thank the professor who had provided him with a letter of introduction to London and was able to help him by rebuilding some astronomical instruments which had been bequeathed to the university in a state of very bad repair. A little later he was invited to set up business as instrument-maker and repairer within the actual grounds of the university.

Within two years his business had so grown that he needed a partner, and he found him in John Craig, an architect with money, who undertook to handle the financial side of the venture. They needed larger premises, so moved outside the university grounds — though Watt went on living there, and doing all the work they required.

Five years later the firm was employing sixteen men and had sales of over £600 a year. There seemed nothing it was unable to do and Watt himself undertook to repair all sorts of toys, as well as violins, flutes and organs. Later he took to building all these things.

He was twenty-seven when he married — and a good catch. On the other hand, he was the least competent of businessmen and might well have got into difficulties after Craig's death the next year: difficulties from which the canny Margaret saved him.

In the year of his marriage he was handed a particularly difficult job: would he repair the university's model of a Newcomen steam engine? It had never worked properly and its recent visit to London for overhaul had made matters worse.

This was a challenge if ever there was one: a challenge not only to James Watt, but to Scotland. He set to work and stripped the little engine, re-assembled it with joints made leak-proof and the boiler enclosed in a heat-resistant wooden box. But even then the engine, with a bellows blowing like mad into the fire-box, gave a few gasping strokes and stopped dead.

At which point we had better stop and have a look at this Newcomen engine. Its designer, Thomas Newcomen, had greatly improved on the work of his predecessors. He had died in 1729, seven years before Watt was born, yet his engine, with very minor modifications made after his death, was still the best thing available in 1763. But it could only be used as a pump: there was no question of rotary motion. Its piston went slowly up and down, powered by atmospheric pressure, and not steam — though steam was needed in the process — while a lever worked by this piston pumped out mine shafts or delivered water through pipes. Newcomen's great innovation had been to provide a separate boiler, and not rely on the slow and wasteful system of heating a boiler with a piston in it, allowing the piston to move as the steam expanded, and then removing the fire so steam condensed back to water and atmospheric pressure forced the piston back again. Newcomen piped his steam into a separate small cylinder with a piston in it. When the piston had been thrust out by the steam pressure, a valve turned off the inlet of steam and at the same time a jet of cold water *inside* the cylinder condensed the steam and let the piston come back under atmospheric pressure. Previous machines (including Newcomen's own, earlier models) had experimented with a jet of water on the *outside* of the cylinder — which obviously took rather longer to have its effect.

Newcomen's engine was, in its day, of the greatest importance: the pumping of water from mines was a vital task, and without that engine, many shafts would have had to be abandoned. Many countries wanted it, and the one installed in France, at Fresnes, was pumping in forty-eight hours as much water as had been raised in a week by fifty horses and twenty men working day and night in shifts.

It did, however, need its two 'engineers' from England, to operate its taps. It was still only a pump. The development of turning its up-and-down, pumping motion into a rotary one — or even of seeing a need to do so — would be Watt's.

He got the university's Newcomen model working and he now

turned to his own engine. He took his 'walk on a fine Sabbath afternoon', to which we referred earlier, and came back to make a separate condenser, for turning used steam back into water. The steam, having done its work, would be piped to this separate vessel, still hot. (And — which was what really mattered — it would leave the cylinder behind it still hot, so that half the next lot of steam didn't turn to water before it did any work.) In this separate condenser it quietly cooled down to water and was led back to the boiler to be used again.

This enormously improved the efficiency of the engine: a given amount of fuel produced a far greater degree of thrust, pumped far more water.

But somehow, something was still wrong. He had studied his steam (knew it was an invisible substance, that the white vapour one saw at the end of the process, the leak from the cylinder — or from the tea kettle — was steam condensed and useless) and he felt there *must* be a way to get his piston back again, without cooling, wasting, his steam.

This next idea came to him (we do not know whether he was walking on a Sabbath or any other day) and he rushed to put it into effect. Now that he had a cylinder which was kept hot, and needed to be kept hot for maximum efficiency, why not enclose it completely in an outer airtight case filled with steam straight from the boiler? Not only would this keep the cylinder hot: a simple arrangement of valves could make steam press against one face of the piston, then the other, returning it to its original position — the job which had originally been done by the atmosphere.

And so, at last, there was a real *steam* engine. The steam provided all the power, was not merely a means of providing a vacuum so that atmospheric pressure did the work.

Oddly enough, the innovation of using all this to provide rotative power, to turn wheels, was left to the last. Watt's next great step forward, which would halve the cost of running a steam engine and increase its efficiency, was expansive working. He found that if he let steam into his cylinder and then shut it off when the piston had travelled only a fraction of its full distance, it would still travel that full distance, with great force, simply because the steam expanded. So 'one wee spoonful of steam' injected alternately on each side of the piston, did what great gusts of steam had done less effectively before.

And at last Watt developed the rotative engine we know today: converting the up-and-down motion into a rotating one. At first, not trusting the time-honoured crank of spinning-machine and foot-lathe, he devised a system whereby a planet wheel, fastened rigidly to a connecting rod on the end of his piston, rotated like a planet round a sun, around a central wheel which was keyed to the shaft that was to be driven.

Ingenious as this was, he discovered that the old spinning-wheel crank — which he had believed too weak for the engine — was better. All his later engines incorporated a crankshaft and a fly-wheel — terms which are familiar to us but which were apologetically introduced by James Watt.

There was one problem left. An engine with a constant speed was highly desirable, yet the steam engine varied its speed with the load imposed. He invented the centrifugal governor, in which the tendency of heavy iron or brass balls to fly outwards when whirled round like chestnuts on a string could be made to narrow the steam inlet and reduce speed.

And this was the final Watt engine: not the first steam engine in history, but as far removed from its predecessors as the rifle from the spear. It had separate condenser, double action, expansive working and a governor. The governor alone, an afterthought by Watt, was a step into something we now call 'automation' — roughly two hundred years ahead of its time. For the first time, a machine could use its own 'intelligence', decide it was running too fast, slow down.

The Watt engine absolutely revolutionized industry. It came in time to operate the new cotton mills and to give power to a new range of metal- and wood-working tools. By linking the crankshaft of Watt's engine through shafting and belts, to all the machinery in a workshop or factory, it could be made to operate drills, lathes, and the rest of the equipment with a speed and an efficiency undreamed of.

But as inventors throughout history have found — the most

brilliant ideas bring little reward until they are completely developed and completely commercial. Watt found himself suddenly a
very poor man: he had devoted so much time — and money — to
his engine that his instrument-making work had suffered.

And how did he re-coup his losses? He used the knowledge of
survey work which he had acquired in repairing survey instruments,
and set himself up as a surveyor. He remained an instrument-
maker, but managed to find some three days a week to do the other
job, and made £200 a year from it, which solved his financial
problem. He surveyed the route of a number of canals, and for his
work on a part of the great Caledonian, from Inverness to Fort
William, he was highly commended by the architect of that scheme,
Thomas Telford.

He remained solvent. But he required the greater opportunities
of England and soon he was able to form a partnership with
Matthew Boulton in Birmingham, a man with wealth and influence,
who was genuinely interested in the inventor and his engine. In May
of 1774 Watt, still only thirty-nine, moved with wife and family to
Birmingham. A few months later the firm of Boulton and Watt was
making steam-engines for sale.

They soon found that while the making of one engine was a
reasonably simple matter, the manufacture of many was highly
complex. For a start, the accurate boring of cylinders took weeks
and was often a failure. The partners were fortunate in getting hold
of a man, whose name is still famous today, who was a brilliant
worker in iron: John Wilkinson, and he was able to turn out the
cylinders with the accuracy required. He took over the supply of all
cylinders to the firm, and when another iron-worker made a bid in
competition, Matthew Boulton wrote back, 'Wilkinson hath bored
us several cylinders almost without error: that of 50" diameter for
Bently & Co. doth not err the thickness of an old shilling in no part,
so you must improve in boring —'

Watt was fortunate in his choice of partner. He himself was
highly strung, temperamental, and quite unable to deal with money
or any sort of crisis — and Boulton, urbane and level-headed, was
the exact opposite. There was a period of depression, which
reached its worst in 1781, and Watt, puzzled and panicky, wanted

to foreclose on all defaulters. Boulton managed to calm him, and by imaginative methods (as far ahead of their time as Watt's governor), like investing money in the defaulting firms to make them solvent, fight their way out of the crisis.

Both Watt and Boulton lived to a ripe old age, and retired in excellent health to hand over to their sons. Boulton died in 1809 at the age of eighty-two, and Watt, still a youngster of seventy-three with another ten years to go, was heart-broken. He wrote Matthew's son, 'Few men have had his abilities and still fewer have exerted them as he has done, and if to them we add his urbanity, his generosity and his affection to his friends, we shall make up a character rarely to be equalled.'

In the closing years of his life James Watt received many honours. He was a Fellow of the Royal Society of Edinburgh, and of the Royal Society in London. The University of Glasgow made him an honorary LL.D. Other countries showered unpronounceable honours upon him. His own offered a baronetcy which he politely refused: 'Sir James Watt? Never.'

His closing years, away from the business — which had worried him — were peaceful and prosperous. Had he been more willing to take risks he would certainly have pioneered the steam locomotive, which would have to wait for someone else — though the hard work had already been done by Watt. Watt's chief interest had been to make the best possible steam engine in the world, and go right on doing that. He succeeded — and the demand for those engines went right on mounting. They gave the spur to the Industrial Revolution, but other factors were already in operation when Watt was completing his model: a transition was taking place from the methods and economics of cottage industry and the domestic workshop on the one hand, to larger-scale factory production on the other. Watt and his machine came at the right time to hasten this.

Today steam sounds out of date, old-fashioned. But it still plays — thanks to that temperamental Scottish genius from Greenock — a very large part in all our lives — for most electricity is generated by steam. We may picture in our mind's eye something like the Aswan Dam in the middle of Britain, producing hydro-electric power — but the fact remains that most electricity in Britain comes from steam-driven generators, even when that steam comes from nuclear fission. (Only the north of Scotland has moved out of the nineteenth century into the next, with its North of Scotland Hydro-Electric Board.) Most power stations now use the fast-running steam turbine, in which high-pressure steam impels a device like a water-wheel: but this would have taken years longer to perfect without James Watt.

And yet — James Watt did a lot more than play with steam. He acquired a vast knowledge, in his spare moments, of architecture, the law, medicine and music. He could, and did, build pipe organs, which he played expertly for the delight of his friends. He became fluent in several languages and was able to link with his Fellowship of the Royal Society the same distinction in the Institute of France. Although he regarded steam as his life's work, he made his mark in other ways. He invented a perspective machine for drawing, and a new type of printing press; he shared with Priestley the discovery that water is a compound of hydrogen and oxygen, and he introduced the novel idea of 'horsepower' as a means of measuring engine output.

He was eighty-four when he died. He had been, as we saw, a sickly child. Perhaps the moral is: work with steam. Certainly inventing television sets and glass razor-blades never did John Logie Baird's health any good.

Before he died, Watt put his own achievement in words, without any false modesty:

'I have spent a long life in improving the arts and manufactures of the nation. My inventions at present, or lately, give employment to the best part of a million of people. Having added many millions to the natural riches, I therefore have a natural right to rest in my extreme old age.'

John Loudon McAdam

The girls of Sussex get their long and lovely legs through pulling them out of the mud.

This 1690 observation — in dead earnest — might have applied to numerous other English counties: and might still apply to them; for though we have roads now, which were lacking in 1690, a few strides off one of them in, say, April, will give ample scope for leg-stretching exercise.

For the fact that we have roads, and good ones, we must thank John McAdam. We have come to take them so much for granted that it requires an effort of reason to consider the bald fact that the Industrial Revolution, despite James Watt and his steam engine, despite every other invention and mechanization, would never have happened at all — without McAdam roads. Without them there could have been no transport of the goods so rapidly, efficiently and cheaply made; no sale for them. Production in England's proud new factories would have stopped almost before it began.

It seems odd that Britain should have been so starved of roads: the Romans left plenty behind, and these, with a little care and maintenance, would have survived into our present day, as indeed some do. But for the most part it is only the names that remain: Watling Street, The Icknield Way, Ermine Street and the rest of them.

The Romans built for ever — and the fact that their handiwork is still with us, two thousand years or so after they did it, seems proof enough that they succeeded. Thomas Telford built roads in the same way and they were superb and extremely expensive. Labour costs had been less in the time of the Romans.

It needed McAdam to work out a way of building roads which was really efficient and yet not prohibitively expensive. Were it not for McAdam we might still, in many ways, be back in the eighteenth century, without its charm. Our various local councils would be arguing whether to leave Piccadilly and Princes Street, Sauchiehall Street and the Mall just muddy cart tracks till the end of time, or float a loan to pave them by Telford's method.

Which is not to denigrate Telford: he was a brilliant engineer, who made everything, and to whom we owe an enormous debt. John McAdam was only the chap who made the road. But we would have been in a bad way without him.

He was the youngest of ten children, born in Ayrshire, in 1756, and descended from landed gentry. Indeed, the family pedigree seems to have embraced the nobility as well, and to be genuinely descended not only from Robert III, King of Scotland, but also from Edward III of England. But by the time Number Ten came along, John Loudon's father's resources were thoroughly strained, and he decided, after much worry and soul-searching, to send the boy to America. There, in an up-and-coming Colony where Mr. McAdam's younger brother was already settled, the lad would stand a chance.

He was fourteen when at last he reached New York, was embraced by Uncle William and introduced to the pleasant world

of minor merchant princes, those eighteenth-century White Sett-
lers of Manhattan. It was a good life, though it would soon be rent
by civil war, the War of American Independence. It would have
been unthinkable for young John Loudon McAdam to have aligned
himself with the rebels, and at the outbreak of hostilities he enlisted
as a volunteer in a Loyalist New York regiment. We know little
about his military service during the Revolution except the established fact that the whole of Manhattan Island and Long Island
remained in English hands throughout the war, and no doubt he did
his bit to ensure this.

As a result of which he and all other Loyalists were understandably in disgrace when the war ended in American victory. By an act
of the Congress, all their properties were attainted and become the
property of the State (exactly as had happened in Scotland with the
properties of men supporting the '15 and the '45). In 1783, John
sailed home to Scotland. He was a man of twenty-seven with a wife
(described on their wedding day, by the *New York Gazette*, as a
'Young Lady of Great Beauty and Merit with a large Fortune') and
their two children. The fortune was gone and prospects in Ayrshire
seemed glum, but they managed somehow to buy themselves a
house and settle down.

And they fell on their feet. As John McAdam's daughter
Georgina was to write, much later, 'My father made many valuable
friends in New York, for owing to the war it was crowded with
officers of rank.... It was fortunate for my parents that the war
sent all home together, and the American set were all very
aristocratic. My father lost nothing, therefore, in point of station in
the world by living so long abroad. He found his sisters in the same
circle that they had always belonged to and as much visited and
made of as ever.'

But McAdam was a remarkable man in his own right, and it was
not entirely the work of his aristocratic friends which placed him as
Deputy-Lieutenant of Ayrshire. The job was no sinecure, for it
involved among other things the raising of a corps of volunteer
artillery to resist the invading French armies whensoever they
might come, and he did it with great enthusiasm.

Field artillery, to be effective, needs roads — and young

volunteer Major McAdam discovered his country had none. None, that is, worthy of the name. They were bad enough in England: in Scotland even the good ones were 'at once loose, rough and perishable, expensive, dangerous to travel on and very costly to repair'.

Oddly enough, though the name McAdam now suggests to us a tarmac road, there was no question during the great road-maker's life of using tar or any other binding substance with the little stones out of which he built a road: yet one of his first business enterprises was a firm that manufactured tar from coal. Three years after his return from New York he and his distant kinsman, the Earl of Dundonald, were partners in the British Tar Co. A by-product of the tar-making was coke, and this was conveniently utilized in making iron at their Muirkirk Iron Co.

Fifteen years of satisfying work, both for himself and for Scotland, ended when he was appointed to Bristol in charge of victualling the Navy.

To his surprise, he found the roads in and around Bristol as inadequate — or absent — as they had been in Ayrshire.

He had, for many years, given thought to methods of constructing a road that would take all sorts of traffic and need the minimum of repair, and he thought now that he had a formula for it. But at first, in Bristol, his suggestions about road-making were dismissed: his job was to victual ships, not waste his time trying to improve communications on land, which had functioned adequately for hundreds of years.

But at last, in 1816, the Bristol Municipality appointed him as its General Surveyor and John Loudon McAdam began his career as a builder of roads. He was sixty years old.

Just what was a McAdam road?

It was not, as we have seen, a thing of bitumen. It differed greatly in fact and in principle from those laid down by Thomas Telford, for McAdam believed that a road should be sprung. Not for him the heavy paving which the Romans and Telford used, upon which they build up their layers of stone and binding: his road should be entirely composed of stones, none of which were more than six ounces in weight, and the total thickness should be in the neighbourhood of ten inches. Laying this directly upon the earth (which, if needed, must be first drained) made it spring when horses and vehicles used it. This, he maintained, gave a smoother journey, and a longer interval between repairs to the surface.

The road should be laid almost flat — not highly cambered as was the practice when he took over the work — with only just enough rise, say three inches in a road eighteen feet across, for the water to run off into the ditches on either side. It should not be a great stone erection, but simply 'an artificial flooring forming a strong, smooth and solid surface at once capable of carrying great weight and over which carriages may pass without meeting any impediment'.

To ensure that his individual pieces of stone — he preferred flint — were no more than six ounces in weight, he devised a two-inch ring measure. If the stone wouldn't go through, it was too big. The stones were broken on site by workmen (and women) sitting down to do the job with little hammers and laying them carefully. Because they were deliberately broken and were not rounded pebbles from a beach, their sharp angles made them unite into a compact mass which was entirely waterproof.

With a road built this way, about ten inches thick — and absolutely without any admixture of earth or chalk or clay or other matter — McAdam maintained any load could be carried. We can condense his own views this way, still keeping the words of a letter he wrote to the President of the Board of Agriculture on the subject:

> The erroneous opinion so long acted upon and so tenaciously adhered to, that by placing a large quantity of stone under the road a remedy will be found for the sinking into wet clay, or other soft soils and the road be made sufficiently strong artificially to carry heavy carriages though the sub-soil be in a wet state, and by such means avert the inconveniences of the natural soil receiving water from rain or other causes, has produced most of the defects of the roads of Great Britain.
>
> It should be well known to every skilful and observant road-maker that if strata of stone of various sizes be placed on a road the largest stones will constantly work up by the shaking and pressure of the traffic, and that the only mode of keeping the stones from motion is to use material of a uniform size from the bottom.

It has been found that roads laid upon a hard bottom wear away more quickly than those which are placed upon a soft soil. It is a known fact that a road lasts much longer over a morass than when made over rock.

The first operation in making a road should be the reverse of digging a trench. The road should not be sunk below but rather raised above the ordinary level of the adjacent ground, and care should be taken that there be a sufficient fall to take off the water. This must be done either by making drains into lower ground, or if that be not practicable from the nature of the country, then the soil upon which the road is proposed to be laid must be raised by addition, so as to be some inches above the level of the water.

Having secured the soil from *under* water the roadmaker should next secure it from rain water by means of a solid road made of clean, dry stone or flint, so selected, prepared and laid so as to be perfectly impervious to water. This cannot be done unless the greatest care be taken that no earth, clay, chalk or other matter that will hold or conduct water be mixed with the broken stone, which must be so prepared and laid as to unite by its own angles into a firm, compact, impenetrable body.

The thickness of such a road is immaterial as to its strength for carrying weight. This object is already attained by providing a dry surface over which the road is to be placed as a covering or roof in order to preserve it in that state, experience having shown that if water passes through and fills the native soil the road, whatever may be its thickness, loses its support and goes to pieces.

None of the new roads I have recently constructed on this principle are more than six inches thick, and although that on the great north road is subjected to very heavy traffic, being only 15 miles distant from London, it has not given way, nor was it affected by the late severe winter, when the roads between that point and London became impassable by breaking up to the bottom. On the roads built according to the system I have described, over 100 miles of them, there was no interruption of travelling, nor any additional expense by the Post Office in conveying mails over them.

There, more or less in a nutshell, we have the recipe for making a good road — for the 'very heavy traffic' on the great north road of the early nineteenth century: and for reasonably light traffic today. McAdam did not live to see the sort of traffic, heavy lorries travelling at fifty and sixty miles an hour, which would have destroyed his road.

But that last sentence in his letter is doubly interesting. He speaks of roads built *according to the system he described* — and he points out that the Post Office had no additional expense in maintaining them, for they needed no repair.

McAdam was becoming an old man and his invention of a revolutionary new method for making roads had earned him, directly, not a penny, although others, all over the land, were using the method. Even the Post Office was saving money, hand over fist. Soon he would ask — much as an inventor of radar would ask, more than a century later — whether a grateful government might not see its way to rewarding him.

Radar is not the sort of device any man can pretend to have invented; a few minutes' cross-examination before an expert committee asking questions about oscilloscopes, scanning, and optimum frequencies, would reduce most of us to a quivering wreck. But any man can build a road if he spends a little time — a very little time — finding out how. Some of us could go out, right now, having digested the recipe above, and assemble a team to make a McAdam road. We could very easily maintain that we had been using that not very complex system for years.

We could say we thought of it first.

And this is exactly what other people did, when John McAdam's case was presented, near the end of his life, to Parliament. Not only was he using other men's ideas; he had made himself a great deal of money as Surveyor in charge of all the roads he had time to supervise himself, and he had brought down his sons from Scotland to share the work and the profit.

The last part is true. McAdam was a good businessman and a good father. When he felt that his own strength was failing and that he would not be able to do all the work he wanted, he sent for his three sons. All of them were able and very soon they were in charge of long stretches of roadmaking all over England — and later Scotland — which rewarded them well. But John himself did a great deal of his work for no reward at all. He was frank about this when a Committee of the House of Commons examined him to see whether he was worthy of any financial grant. The chairman asked him why he had maintained in evidence that, had he charged for his advice, it would have hindered the introduction of his system, and McAdam replied:

'I form that opinion because in every case when I was written to for advice or assistance, it was preceded by a letter desiring to know what the expense would be. Upon coming to every Trust I afterwards found there was a party adverse to my being consulted — I found they had always opposed my being sent for under the pretence that it would be an enormous expense. In any case, they never consented to my being sent for until a letter came from me to say it would be no expense at all.... My belief is that if I had made it a money-making speculation I should have strangled the business at its birth and my system never would have been introduced in the country at all.'

McAdam did succeed in getting grants in recognition of what he had done, but to the end of his life he was opposed and misrepresented. Then, and later, he was compared unfavourably with Thomas Telford, a great and uncomplicated man who was as different from John Loudon McAdam as it is possible to imagine. Telford was the genial bachelor who lived for engineering, had no home life and didn't want any; whereas McAdam was a businessman and a family man and he insisted he was no engineer, just a maker of roads. There seems little evidence that the two men ever quarrelled, but their supporters did, and baseless rumours flourished about the remarks each was said to have made about the other. The poet Southey waxed lyrical about Telford, called him *Pontifex Maximus* — and dismissed the other man's work as quackadamizing. Someone else thought up the title 'Colossus of Roads' for McAdam and dismissed Telford as his inferior.

But while all this was going on, Britain was getting roads. A few years back even London had been almost a beleaguered city in the winter. Lord Hervey had written from Kensington to a friend complaining that 'the road between this place and London is grown so infamously bad that we live here in the same solitude as if cast on a rock in the middle of the ocean. All Londoners tell us that between them and us there is an impassable gulf of mud.'

All this was becoming a thing of the past, thanks to McAdam. (The Telford road was too expensive, took too long to build, for anything other than main highways.) Slowly the streets and squares of London were being macadamized, and one great advantage of the innovation was that the roadway was not only free of mud and potholes, but almost silent when carriages and horses went over it. *The Times* wrote:

> The Vestry of St. James's parish have, with a view of lessening the noise of carriages during Divine Service, Macadamized that part of Jermyn Street which adjoins the Church.'

The heavy paving stones which had been issued in London, apart from their tendency to sink into the earth, made a dismal clatter when wheels or hooves went over.

Seldom has the name of a process been so swiftly absorbed into the language. A music critic was soon to complain of a virtuoso's 'macadamizing a few broad, simple and impressive sounds into passages of numberless rapid notes —' A bishop was described as having 'macadamized the way for his successor'; suitors tried to 'macadamize' young women into conversation; the poet Thomas Hood sends out 'a gondolier on smooth macadam seas'.

Hood, in fact, sets out the road-builder's claims to fame quite succinctly during his lengthy *Ode to Mr. McAdam*:

> *Dispenser of coagulated good,*
> *Distributor of granite and of food!*
> *Long may thy fame its even path march on*
> *E'en when thy sons are dead,*
> *Best benefactor! Though thou giv'st a stone*
> *To those who ask for bread!*

In 1836, returning in his eighty-first year from his annual visit to Scotland, McAdam was taken ill and died.

If ever proof had been needed of the service he and his sons were giving in their careful supervision of the McAdam process, it was available, in abundance, after he died. Within a year or two roads were built all over Britain which paid lip-service to their inventor and were a travesty of the process. Stones of all sizes were being used, the roadway was being filled with earth and clay, drainage was being neglected.

The reason, one astute observer pointed out, was 'ignorant vestries in league with corrupt contractors'.

And here we have another clue to the real service John McAdam gave his country. From the very first days in Bristol he had noticed that contractors and sub-contractors needed constant supervision by honest surveyors. He and his sons gave that supervision, and the roads were a monument to them. They died — and the process almost died with them.

But they left behind them thousand upon thousand of miles of superb road across the face of the world. We no longer make our highways that way — but McAdam's roads fulfilled an urgent need. No motorway of the future can ever be half as important.

Thomas Telford

A Scot who would have qualified for a place in this book had there been more space is Samuel Smiles. He was a remarkable man, educated for the medical profession in Edinburgh University and then tossing the idea, the training, away to become social reformer and writer.

There was no doubt in his mind; he had waded through years of medical studentship and found himself wanting; his interests lay elsewhere. Wisely, courageously, he set about doing something else.

This is a point which has often exercised me: how many of us start off in the wrong lane and have neither the courage nor the opportunity to get into the right one? How many doctors, dentists, should have been actors, bus conductors, fabric designers, head waiters? How many airline pilots should have been hairdressers or plumbers?

We will never know.

One thing that started me thinking along these cynical lines years ago was the immediate post-war period when I persuaded the RAF to teach me, a soldier, how to fly. There was a large course of us, all young, dead keen and obviously with an interest in flying.

In the first few weeks the penguins and the eagles were separated; the penguins, who had failed to go solo in the required number of flying hours, crept back to their units. The rest of us, proud and confident, settled down to a few months' hard work.

A few more dropped, winged, by the wayside. I nearly did myself, being unable to land an aeroplane in the dark, so that I went round and round, missing the flare-path, the runway, each time. Then, a panicky realization that I might run out of fuel and plunge down a factory chimney, got me down, and alive.

But I wasn't the worst. Not by a long chalk. I was a typical young man of the sort who takes up flying, with a wild urge to get airborne, and some aptitude for it — like everyone else on the course. And half of us would have been better off doing something quite different; though most of us were good enough to survive and get wings.

But if I thought today that any one of us — with the exception of, say, three — anyone from the distant Operational Training Unit, or anyone *like* them, was up in front in the Boeing Jet or the Concorde — or the Piper Cub — on which I had booked a seat, I would disembark in haste.

And, of course, by the law of averages, somebody just like that *would* be there. For until someone devises a foolproof system of putting us all in the right slot we will go on having pilots who ought to have been ballet dancers or shoe salesmen; doctors who should have been airline pilots, or journalists, or bricklayers.

And engineers who should have been put on to something very, very different.

We digressed because of Samuel Smiles, a man who had the courage and the commonsense to switch his horses in mid-stream. And one of Smiles's greatest works, of which we would have been deprived had he remained a saw-bones, is *Lives of the Engineers*.

One of his *Lives*, Thomas Telford, is that rarest of birds, the man who could never have been anything other than what he was — a dedicated, brilliant, civil engineer. Perhaps Smiles, an exact opposite, understood him better than most.

He tells us Thomas Telford was born in 'one of the most solitary nooks of the narrow valley of the Esk, in the eastern part of the county of Dumfries, in Scotland'. The year was 1757, and 'before the year was out he was an orphan'. His father, a hardworking shepherd, died in November, leaving a widow and the infant Thomas.

The house they lived in was little more than a mud hut, but as all who study Scotland know, this made no difference at all to the boy's opportunities for education. There was — as there always is — an excellent village school, which he attended until he was fourteen. And by this time he had no doubts at all — he would become an engineer.

First, though, he would allow himself to be apprenticed to a mason. This was a disaster, for the man disliked Telford as much as Telford disliked the man, and the young apprentice ran home to his mother. But as the work was what he wanted, he helped his mother look round for another placing and at last was happily settled with Andrew Thomson at Langholm.

At first there was little masonry to be done, and the early months of apprenticeship were frustrating. Young Thomas Telford was put to every other sort of building task but that of mason. The reason was straightforward: in Telford's own words, the houses round about consisted of 'one storey of mud walls, or rubble stones bedded in clay, and thatched with straw, rushes or heather; the floors being of earth and the fire in the middle, while instead of windows small openings in the thick mud walls admitted a scanty light'.

Fortunately for Andrew Thomson and his apprentice, a new Duke of Buccleugh inherited the land for miles around. He was a young man, full of ideas, and he set about repairing and rebuilding every house on his property. Mud would be replaced by stone, straw by slate.

Soon the masons had all the work they could handle, and Telford realized that this sort of building, not for today or tomorrow, but for posterity, was the only work that interested him. There was no overtime rate in those days, but he went on working long after his employer had downed chisel for the night, lovingly shaping and facing the stones. He finished his apprenticeship but stayed on with Thomson because there was still so much work to do. Then, aged twenty-two, he headed for Edinburgh.

But before he did, he cut a headstone for his father's grave. It had been marked with only a small cairn for those twenty-two years, and now he lovingly chiselled out:

> *In Memory of*
> *John Telford*
> *Who after living 33 years*
> *an Unblameable Shepherd*
> *Died at Glendinning*
> *November 1757*

Edinburgh, for a poor boy from the country, was like one of the wonders of the world. He got work, all he could manage, rebuilding the capital of fine stone. He spent what spare time he had moving about the town, studying the buildings, the castle, Holyrood House.

But after two years, 'I considered that my native country afforded few opportunities of exercising my profession to any extent. I therefore judged it advisable (like many of my countrymen) to proceed southward, where industry might find more employment, and be better remunerated.'

Telford, in fact, is setting out, in his own words, the theme of this book.

He set out on horseback, and when he arrived, weeks later, it was to find, as he had hoped, that there was a great deal of work and very few masons to do it. An elderly spinster from his village, who had let him read books in her small library, had also armed him with a letter. This got him into the presence of no less a man than Sir William Chambers, architect of Somerset House. He got work on that building, which kept him in reasonable comfort at his lodgings, for wages were good; but each evening he busied himself drawing plans for buildings of his own.

We can say right now that Thomas Telford, though he was unquestionably one of Britain's greatest engineers, was a very lucky man. Perhaps a part of that luck stemmed from his attractive personality, for men and women liked him as soon as they met him, were anxious to help him. And though he would soon be in little need of it, a young civil engineer (qualified only as stone mason) needs all he can get. He was befriended by Sir William Pulteney, who gave him two commissions: he was to prepare plans for major alterations to Pulteney's large house, and to carry out the rebuilding of a vicarage on his property.

He did the jobs well, and prospered by them. He met the Adam brothers, much-travelled, well-off architects from his native land, and they were fascinated by this rough but charming man who told them, 'There is nothing done in stone or marble that we cannot do in the completest manner.'

This first person plural seems to have embraced the partner he hoped to take in with him, but that plan came to nothing. For most of a busy life Thomas Telford worked by himself. He travelled to Portsmouth where he spent another two years, part of them building a house for the Dockyard Commissioner. Already his name as one of the finest masons in Britain had spread to most of Britain's towns. But his chief interest in Portsmouth was studying the harbour, the docks.

There was a lull in the work and once again good fortune smiled upon him. His old friend Pulteney, delighted with the work on mansion and vicarage, was now able to organize a really important job for him, that of County Surveyor in Shropshire.

This was wonderful: he had been tacitly accepted as both architect and engineer, and he flung himself into the job. He found — and it pleased him — that much of it would involve bridges and bridging, for Shropshire is a land of rivers. His first bridge, though he had amused himself by planning many over the years, was at Montford, to the west of Shrewsbury. It would carry the main London-Holyhead road over the Severn, and although Telford did not know it at the time, this road and its bridges would always be associated with his name.

But in the meantime, as the Montford bridge was abuilding under his instructions, he had one of those rare 'I told you so' experiences which, when they come, give such sardonic joy. As County Surveyor he was asked to inspect the old church of St. Chad in Shrewsbury town. To the anger and dismay of the churchwardens he submitted a report stating that the edifice was highly unsafe: graves had been dug so close to the foundations that it was in danger of toppling over. A patching job on the roof — which was what the wardens had in mind — would be a waste of time and money, until the walls were made safe.

The report was rejected as too expensive and unnecessary. A local builder was put on to the patching.

And the next morning, as the builder's men stood outside the church, while someone went off to get a key, it happened. There was a thunderous crash and most of the church dissolved into ruins.

'The very parts I had pointed out were those which gave way, and down tumbled the tower, forming a very remarkable ruin, which astonished and surprised the vestry and roused them from their infatuation, although they have not yet recovered from the shock.'

Telford's first bridge was of stone, but his second effort is of greater importance, for he built it of iron. It was not only efficient, but beautiful, having one long, slender span. The reason for having only one was Telford's belief that river traffic on the Severn (for this was another bridge over that river) must not be interefered with. And, though he could hardly have known it, waterways would concern him a great deal.

Canals in England were almost exactly Telford's age: he had been an infant when the first one was dug from the Worsley coal pits to Manchester. And we can skip a bridge or two to move to the next stage in Telford's career, the planning, designing, of canals.

Canals, in those days of bad roads and no railways, were the hope of the future. Nothing — not even the good roads which Telford would soon be building — would be able to carry large cargoes like coal economically. And so men began to dig them, and the navigating engineers, the 'navvies', who did it, have left us a picturesque

name for something quite different. Telford's first canal was the
Ellesmere, joining the Mersey, the Severn and the Dee and linking
Liverpool overland with Bristol. It was a daunting task, for there
were high hills, deep valleys, to cross. The age-old method had been
to build locks which would enable small barges to be lifted up, in
the water which floated them, and be placed, water and all, on a
higher level. (And, going down the hill, lowered gently in reverse.)
The process was and is much like lifting a minnow from a stream in
a bucket and gently pouring minnow and water into a tub. But the
closing of the lock, and the slow raising or lowering of it, is a time-
consuming process. To negotiate one of the valleys on the proposed canal route would have necessitated a total of sixteen locks:
eight down to the floor of the valley; another eight up again, on the
far side. Getting a barge or a narrowboat through this chain might
easily take a day — and the horizontal distance was only half a mile.

So he planned — and built — an aqueduct.

It was a remarkable feat of engineering. There have been man-
made rivers lifted up on stilts to negotiate an obstacle, but none like
Telford's at Pontcysylte. It took eight years to build. The iron
river-bed was lifted a hundred and twenty-seven feet, and carried on
nineteen pillars. For the first seventy feet of their height these were
solid: above that, hollow. The cast-iron trough they supported was
seven and a half feet wide, with a four and a half feet towpath beside
it.

The canal was finished in 1803 and the two aqueducts, Pontcysylte and the smaller Chirk which Telford built simultaneously,
are its outstanding landmarks. To Walter Scott, the former was
'the most impressive work of art' he had ever seen.

It deserved to be. From this moment on Thomas Telford's name
was world-famous.

There were more canals, more aqueducts, more bridges. And in
1801, while the Ellesmere was being finished to his plans, he was
asked to tour the highlands of Scotland and advise on the possi-
bility of getting better fishing harbours on the west coast; naval
bases on the east; and a canal right across the country from east
coast to west.

As always, he plunged into the job, made recommendations,

many of them sweeping, most of which were gratefully accepted. Telford did more for communications in Scotland than any man before him — or perhaps since. He planned no less than 1,200 bridges, all of which were built to his instructions. He charted nine hundred and twenty miles of major road, all of which was laid down.

And he built the Caledonian Canal.

It was a brilliantly executed piece of engineering, which got him commissions from all over Europe and, among other things, a Swedish knighthood. But commercially, it was a failure.

The fault was not Telford's. The Caledonian Canal was made obsolete, almost before it was finished, by the coming of steam.

The plan behind it, of course, had been avoidance of a long haul for sailing vessels, right over the top of Scotland. These, when work began, were the only ships in existence, and it was not uncommon for them to take weeks, battling with alternate storm and dead calm, to get from the east coast to the west — from North Sea to Atlantic Ocean. But by the time the canal was finished, steam ships were almost commonplace; one of these could dash over the top of Scotland in a day or so, without worrying about winds.

But it was still an astonishing feat of engineering.

It was sixty miles long — and there were others far longer than this in existence. But it was a ship canal, not a midget waterway for barges, and Telford designed it 110 feet wide on the surface, narrowing to 50 feet at its bottom, 20 feet below. The locks — for no aqueduct would be possible on this scale — were watertight chambers 180 feet by 40, and 20 feet in depth. Telford designed and built twenty-eight of these to cover the distance, including sea locks at each end which were miniature harbours.

He was sixty-five when the Caledonian Canal opened: it had taken nineteen years, from 1803 to 1822. But in the meantime he had accomplished other near-miracles. He had built splendid harbours at Aberdeen and at Wick (and made alterations to fifty others); he had built, for Sweden, the Gotha Canal linking the Baltic to the North Sea, exactly twice the length of his Caledonian; he had started work on the great bridge over the Menai Strait, linking the mainland of Wales with the Isle of Anglesey. Its purpose, of course, was, and still is, to speed up the journey from

England to Ireland, via the steamer crossing at Holyhead. Telford's job was not only to throw a huge suspension bridge (one of history's first) across the Strait, but to build or re-build countless others, to make miles of road, to alter gradients, the whole way from London to Holyhead.

The Menai Bridge took seven years to build. Before it began, Telford carried out tests on the tensile strength of iron, opened up special quarries for the stone. He built his bridge with a span of 550 feet (unheard of, in those days) between two supporting pillars, and clearing high water by 100 feet. It had two carriageways 12 feet wide, with a central pathway 4 feet wide. The first London-Holyhead mail coach passed from the mainland to Anglesey on 30 January, 1826, with a beaming Telford following in a post-chaise.

One might call this superb bridge the Monument to Telford. But there are Telford roads and Telford bridges all over Britain — and in many parts of Europe, including Russia, as well as his canals. Perhaps his most beautiful bridge was the one over the Clyde at Broomielaw, a bridge without steel this one, with seven stone arches and a total length of 560 feet. It was also, at 60 feet, the widest bridge in Britain when it was completed — but Telford never lived to see that day.

What sort of a man was this *Pontifex Maximus*, as the Poet-Laureate Southey called him, this Master Bridge-builder?

He was a confirmed bachelor, to the day he died. As we said at the beginning, he was an engineer born to the job, for he liked working, living on the site, and until he was sixty-four he never possessed a home of his own. He used as base throughout most of his life a coffee-house near Charing Cross in London, where he had rooms. Samuel Smiles tells the story in his *Lives of the Engineers* that the sight of the great engineer seated in an armchair in the coffee-house began to mean a great deal in daily takings. So much so that when the place changed hands, as it did many times during Telford's residence, he was included, as we would say today, in fixtures and fittings. When Telford at last decided to take a house of his own, and gave notice, 'The landlord, who had but recently entered into possession, stood almost aghast. "What, leave the house!" said he, "why, sir, I have just paid £750 for you!'

And so he had: the man before had paid a mere £450, but Telford had grown in importance. But he left and settled at a house, No. 24 Abingdon Street. He still travelled extensively, going annually to the highlands to inspect his work, but Abingdon Street remained home until his death on 2 September, 1834.

He was, perhaps, a lonely man. He never had any interest in marriage and he seems to have had few relatives. He left all his money to charity. But he had many friends, and he was always eager to meet and help young civil engineers. He had no enemies, despite the tales that he disagreed violently with John Loudon McAdam. His disagreement was one of principle, and a major engineering principle, too, but there was no personal animosity. Perhaps the two men were so totally different in background and outlook that they could never have quarrelled. They were never near enough.

What was this difference of principle?

Telford built for ever: McAdam for the immediate future. Telford's roads were expensive, works of craftsmanship which had borrowed much from the Romans. His road might be anything up to five feet deep, with big stones at the bottom, carefully fitted together, the whole rising through smaller, but still tailored, stones to the surface. McAdam's roads were simpler, and, in fact, he sincerely believed that a soft bottom and nothing but six-ounce stones above it, the whole way through, would last longer. Perhaps it did — but the McAdam road, though its name has lingered, is of little use in today's heavy vehicular traffic.

Telford's roads, had they been wide enough, could have lasted for ever, wherever he laid them — as, in the highlands, many of them will. His canals today take little traffic, but times may change and bring them back to popularity. But his hundreds of bridges, from mighty stone castles to his 'little spider's webs in the sky', remain his monument.

George Gordon Byron, Lord Byron

Byron lay, Lazily Lay
Hid from Lesson and Game Away,
Dreaming Poetry, all Alone –

So we sang, and they sing, at Harrow. Like most school songs, the words of this one were capable of infinite, *sotto voce*, variation; and Byron, during the course of four longish stanzas, could be put in the strangest of situations, without being able to protest. Which was as well, for, as we knew, he was a hot-tempered chap, who throughout his life carried two small loaded pistols.

And now I must stop involving others: I have no idea at all whether my school friends had read all or any of Byron. I myself had read scarcely a word, but his story fascinated me. He seemed so colourful, there was no need for him to have written anything.

We have our mini-Byrons today.

But Byron did write, and though his physical beauty, his title, his wealth, his sexual excess and his spirit of rebellion would have earned him a small place in history somewhere between George the Fourth and Marlon Brando, only the written word could improve on that placing. And Byron wrote like an angel.

He knew, too, the power of words:

> *Words are things, and a small drop of ink,*
> *Falling like dew upon a thought, produces*
> *That which makes thousands, perhaps millions, think;*
> *'Tis strange, the shortest letter which man uses,*
> *Instead of speech, may form a lasting link*
> *Of ages; to what straits old Time reduces*
> *Frail man, when paper – even a rag like this –*
> *Survives himself, the tomb, and all that's his.*

The words are from Byron's *Don Juan*, Canto III. Seldom has poet written a better epitaph for himself.

Perhaps he was the greatest of all the English Romantic poets, greater than Shelley, Wordsworth, Keats. Which, for one who spent so many of his formative years in the north of Scotland, is quite an achievement.

The English, as all good Scotsmen know, are perfidious. Eight years before his death he had been almost literally thrown out of their country, for Breaking the Eleventh Commandment, for Being Found Out. English society, in one of those moods of strait-laced virtue which alternate with periods of astonishing licence, had drummed him out, and at Dover a huge gawking crowd of Englishmen and women, some shaking their fists, others grinning with a frank admiration which none dared put into words, watched him embark with his retinue.

And eight years later when he died — romantically, if a little pointlessly — in Greece, all England wept. Howls of anguish rent the air, the papers, choking back their tears, pointed out for their readers, who already knew, that Byron's death 'came upon London like an earthquake'. A bright light, a beacon, the rest of it, had gone out —

Little Alfred Tennyson, aged fifteen, galloped weeping into a wood to scratch three words on a rock: 'Byron is dead.'

And so he was. But what on earth was there about the man to occasion these violent shifts of public opinion?

He had spent his earliest, most formative, years in Aberdeen. The foundations of his education, his love of words, of mountain beauty, even of Scripture, were laid there, at school and from his nurse. And from that nurse, May Gray, he learnt more than that: the odd devotion they shared was to alter Byron's emotional orientation for ever.

He was grandson of another remarkable man, Admiral John Byron, who had been shipwrecked on the west coast of Patagonia and held prisoner for three years before returning to England in 1745. He too was a writer of sorts, for his *Voyage Round the World* has been extensively read, studied, translated. His son, the poet's father, was a captain in the Guards, and a splendidly potent womanizer.

And we must mention one other antecedent: the fifth Lord Byron was the poet's great-uncle. From him, in the fullness of time, would descend the title which would so endear him to English society; and indeed to the inhabitants of France, Italy, Greece. Even Scotland.

He was born of this stock, and with a Scottish heiress for mother. The year was 1788. Catherine Gordon was related — all Scotsmen have pedigrees — to the Stuart kings. Already his father had squandered her fortune and left her in a small furnished room off Cavendish Square in London, to bear her child.

He was born with a club foot.

Almost immediately Catherine took him home to Aberdeenshire. There, as he grew older, the boy absorbed a stern Scots education, and grew to love wild Highland scenery. (He spent much time around Ballater.) He also learned to love — in a decidedly precocious way — his young nanny.

After ten years of this he learnt his great-uncle's title was now his. 'The Wicked Lord', men had called him, and with reason; for his morals, his profligacy, were as renowned in their way as George's one day would be. The Wicked Lord was dead. George had inherited not only the title, but the family seat in Nottinghamshire, Newstead Abbey.

This, though it was in an alarming state of disrepair, still had an income to go with it. Byron and his mother made haste to move there.

From Newstead he was sent to a preparatory school at Dulwich, thence in 1801 to Harrow. He was thirteen.

He hated it at first. Discipline was strict and most of the classroom subjects were a crashing bore. And there were no women. Somehow he managed to endure it, and Harrow too endured four years of mutual acquaintanceship. But towards the end of these years he was not only enjoying the opportunities for reading which the school gave him, he was astonishing his friends by deeds of schoolboy bravery — a gallant attempt to overcome the handicap of a crippled foot. He made friends here, and later, at Trinity College, Cambridge. He seemed obsessed with a desire for love. Not mere sensuality, which he displayed later, but emotional love, and he directed it at school friends, university friends, his cousin Mary Chaworth during the holidays. He shocked some, amused others.

At Cambridge he struck up an emotional relationship with John Edleston, while at the same time excelling at boxing, riding, swimming. By now he knew he was handsome, even beautiful, that this outweighed the physical disability of his foot; the consideration, the balancing, of these two attributes occupied a great deal of his life.

He did little work, but made strenuous efforts to keep his weight down, keep his perfect profile unmarred by lines, his hair thick and black. The effort was needed, for Byron at Cambridge drank, gambled and womanized to a degree at which we mere twentieth-century men can only marvel. On more than one occasion, so much did youth and beauty obsess him, he signed the Age column in an hotel register as 100. He made sick little jokes when he walked across a room and showed his hated limp. He practised daily with the two pistols he carried everywhere. But, apart from good friends, he derived little benefit from the ancient establishment: his record at Cambridge is merely one of dissolute living and a mounting tide of debt.

So far in this tale there is little for us to study. But now, in 1807, comes the first sign of a genius which has been there all along. In that year he publishes — he is nineteen — a volume of poems, *Hours of Idleness*. Many like it, some do not. Some do not even like *Poems Original and Translated* of the following year. The *Edinburgh Review* dismisses all of it loftily, and this provokes his *English Bards and Scottish Reviewers* in 1809, where he satirizes the Editor — and yet manages to say a great deal, favourable and otherwise, about *English Bards*.

In this year he came of age. He had already received his inheritance, had taken his seat in the House of Lords. Now he would go with his latest, closest friend, John Hobhouse, on The Grand Tour.

They went, and visited Portugal and Spain, thence via Malta and Greece to Albania. From Albania Byron went back to Greece, which exercised a fascination for him, and there he began the long autobiographical poem, *Childe Harold's Pilgrimage* which would soon bring him the most astonishing fame. (In fact, he began it under the title *Childe Burun's Pilgrimage*, then decided against such blatant autobiography.) In the second year of his tour he visited the Middle East and in particular Constantinople. We have seen that he was a good, strong swimmer, and now, to prove it, prove himself equal to the heroes of antiquity, he swam the two miles across the Dardanelles — swam from Asia to Europe. He also found time to finish Canto I and II of *Childe Harold*. He wrote *Hints from Horace* and *The Curse of Minerva*. All these were published after his return to Europe, and *Childe Harold's Pilgrimage*, appearing in February, 1812, took London by storm. Its author was just twenty-four, and 'awoke one morning and found myself famous'. This was an age when poetry really struck to the heart, whether it be frankly romantic, like 'Music arose with its voluptuous spell, Soft eyes looked love to eyes which spake again' (from Byron's *Waterloo*), or adventurous like Scott's. Nothing in our day has struck anything like the same chord, with the tiny, tinkling exception of Dylan Thomas's *Under Milk Wood*.

Byron's gratification at being suddenly famous was marred by the death of his mother. She had died at Newstead before he was able to get back to her, and he never forgave himself. They had quarrelled often — in a frightening way, for they both had terrible tempers and the good lady drank to excess — but he was heartbroken when she died.

For a short time he began to be seen as a rising young statesman. He made a few remarkable speeches in the House of Lords, delivered them in his beautiful voice (his strongest subject at Harrow had been 'Declamation') and brought tears to many a noble eye with his support of Nottingham weavers. Outside the House, indeed everywhere he went, for the beauty and the crippled foot were alike unmistakable, he was fawned on like royalty.

But in 1813 he chanced to re-meet his half-sister. His profligate father, before ruining Catherine Gordon, had been briefly married to the Marchioness of Carmarthen and the daughter of that union had always held a strange attraction for Byron. She was now Mrs. Augusta Leigh; she returned his affection and there seems little doubt that he began an incestuous affair with her.

But not content with this, he began a simultaneous affair with Lady Caroline Lamb. He was at the height of his fame — his *Corsair* of Oriental Tales had sold ten thousand copies on day of publication — and what might have been ignored in a lesser man became society's chief topic of conversation. Never reticent, the poet discussed his amours with all who cared to listen, and Augusta, already trying to break a relationship which would soon be a major scandal, was horrified to learn its details, no doubt magnified, from some good friend who, like all this sort of good friend, felt she ought to know what was being said.

So the horrified Augusta was one of several women who decided to marry Byron off, but fast, before other reputations as well as his own had been compromised. The girl chosen was Miss Annabella Milbanke. A blue-stocking perhaps, but with charm. And — which perhaps clinched the deal — a sizeable fortune of her own. A marriage was arranged. Byron, while perfectly aware of the reasons for matrimony, procrastinated and changed his mind for many, many months. Then, in a flash, the deed had been done.

The marriage lasted a year and there are probably more conflicting tales about that one year of matrimony than of any other union in history. It is quite possible that the marriage, though dull, was successful for most of those twelve months: on the other hand, Byron is supposed to have told his Annabella, on their wedding day, that now he had married her he hated her.

Whatever he told her, she was soon taking medical advice about him, believing and hoping that he was temporarily insane. The doctors refuted this, and as by now the scandal about Augusta Leigh was at its height she planned to leave him.

Right after the birth of their only child, a daughter, she did so and fled to her parents.

It was, for London, the biggest scandal on record. Within a week *Childe Harold* and the rest of Byron's work, all of which women had swooned over, was forgotten. There were few to defend Byron — these only materialized like Robert Edgecombe and his *Byron, the Last Phase*, many years after the man was dead — and many to blame him. There was a separation which was legally satisfactory, and it seems that Byron was genuinely shocked and sorry that his wife had left him. But London society howled for blood. He was ostracized — and yet dragged into functions where he could be publicly disgraced, like Lady Jersey's party. There he was cut by almost everyone, including all his old 'friends'.

And on 25 April, 1816 — fifteen months after contracting marriage — he sailed from Dover, never to return again. As we have seen, there were those at the dock, several rows of them, waiting to sneer. Many great ladies, unwilling to be recognized in the crush, borrowed their maids' clothes to do so.

Probably Byron had an intention at the back of his mind that some day he would return. But he never did.

More problems — most of his own manufacture — now assailed him. He fled in the grand manner, no midnight flit for Lord Byron, and among his entourage was a young and faintly ridiculous Italian doctor, Polidori. No mysterious affection here — merely that Byron, as was often the custom, felt he would require a reliable doctor with him on his travels. Polidori appeared to Byron's publisher, John Murray, to be sufficiently intelligent and trustworthy to be entrusted with a commission: if he kept an exact record of their travels, he, Polidori, would earn five hundred guineas.

The doctor managed to produce a record and collect his five hundred guineas, though his service with Byron ended temporarily when the poet found him too boring. Our only interest in Polidori is in the words which were cut from the first chapter of his journal. These were ultimately replaced by an editor less prudish. The party, according to Polidori, had arrived at Ostend and gone to the hotel, whereupon,

'As soon as he reached his room, Lord Byron fell like a thunderbolt upon the chambermaid.'

And so it was to go on, right across the continent of Europe, with chambermaids, merchants' wives, countesses, all collapsing under him, and one unfortunate — but very foolish — English girl joining their number. She was the poet Shelley's sister-in-law, Claire, who joined Shelley's quite different continental entourage for the sole purpose of pursuing Byron into Italy. She had an illegitimate child by him and was then utterly and cruelly rejected. The child, Allegra, was born in 1817 and kept in a convent by her father. He felt some affection for the little thing, but none for the mother, and was shocked and distressed when Allegra died at the convent, aged five.

Much of the remainder of Byron's life was spent in Venice, where the pattern of chambermaids, grooms' wives and the nobility was maintained. The longest period of fidelity in that life was the four years from 1819 after he had met and wooed the Countess Teresa Guiccioli. She remained his mistress throughout that period. He went on writing — as he always did, faithful or no — and his masterpiece, *Don Juan*, took shape slowly, in Italy. He worked at other poems, *Mazeppa, Sardanapalus, The Prophecy of Dante*. The work was by no means all introspective and he seized on all sorts of different subjects: *The Island, or Christian and his Comrades*, was based on the mutiny aboard H.M.S. *Bounty*, which was then only about thirty years in the past.

He led an active life by day, whether it be philandering, or taking violent exercise out of doors, and much of his writing was done in the evenings. Night after night — or at any rate, on some nights — he wrote stanza after stanza of delightful verses, lubricating his imagination with gin and water. Often the gin and water was the only thing he consumed during the day, for he was vain till the end, and fighting a steady battle with age and obesity.

He had always, since strange distant days in the English House of Lords, taken a lively interest in world affairs, and in particular the question of Greek independence. There had always been the urge to do something about it, not just write on the subject. At last, feeling time slip by, with so many friends fallen by the wayside — Shelley had just been tragically drowned and he had helped cremate the fishgnawed body on the beach — he set off for Greece. Already he had given help to that country's cause, with money, advice, propaganda.

What he thought his actual presence could do is not clear, but he arrived at Missolonghi in January of 1824. The Greeks were naturally overjoyed that so famous a man should so publicly have come to their aid. But by now a lifetime of dissipation — and also overwork, for he never spared himself, in love or labour — was fast catching up. It is almost as if he knew his days were numbered, that he must go out in a blaze of glory, a rebel as ever, supporting the fine cause of independence for a nation from whom the whole of western civilization had sprung.

Perhaps the behaviour of those he befriended speeded the process: the Greeks were fighting absurdly among themselves, and there was no concerted plan, however much he might try to impose one. Greed and jealousy ruled supreme. Byron fell ill — and in his weakened, dissipated state his body could do nothing about it. On 19 April, 1824, he died, in his thirty-sixth year.

The news took a month to reach England. And then, as we have seen, the land which had banished him wailed piteously, beat its breast.

It is pointless to take up a moral stance about Byron. Almost everything he did was morally deplorable. He used women and discarded them cruelly; did the same with men when their use, their attraction, whatever it might be, was over. And still he was almost universally loved — and not only for his poetry. His self-imposed exile had been occasioned by a wave of English self-righteousness, and when that wave had vanished out to sea, in the wake of his own departure (probably even as he fell upon the Ostend chambermaid) a new love welled up for him.

It would have been impossible to write about Byron without discussing him as a flesh and blood man. Which, paradoxically, has been quite the wrong way. For this — this randy peer — would not have survived a generation in men's memory, were it not for what he wrote. And *pace* Ernest Hemingway, who at least pretended to believe no man can write of what he hasn't physically experienced, there is seldom much connection between a writer as the world sees him and a writer as he writes.

There are plenty to drink to Lord Byron, who have never read a dozen lines of his work: but the man they cheer is nothing. It has been a joy writing about His Lordship. But to understand the first thing about him you must close this book, forget everything you have read in it, and start reading what Byron wrote.

(Like this, perhaps, from *Don Juan*:

> *'But I am half a Scot by birth,*
> *And bred a whole one; and my heart*
> *Flies to my head.'*)

David Livingstone

Everyone in this book is, I suppose, 'famous'. Some are goodies, a few perhaps are baddies, and we are concerned only with their achievement. Mary Garden is in these pages because she was a superb artist and gave the greatest joy to thousands of people; Fleming discovered penicillin; Baird invented television so that millions of people —

Never mind. The fact is, they did the things, they were interesting as people. Beyond that, it is probably none of my business or yours to pry.

But almost alone of the assembled men in these pages there is one who was above all else a good man, whose claim to attention lies as much with the fact that he was good as that he happened to discover a lot of Africa.

He was in many ways as near a saint as makes no difference. But he, too, as we shall see, had his faults.

He was born on 19 March, 1813, in Blantyre on the Clyde, in the street Shuttle Row where his entire family lived in a single room fourteen feet by ten. The accommodation had been built for cotton-factory workers by a paternal industrialist, and though the conditions would be unthinkable today, they were regarded as decent in 1813: Blantyre was a model village.

At ten, young David started work in the cotton factory, marching about and tying up the broken threads on the jenny. His hours were from six in the morning to eight at night, after which he attended classes. But no opportunity passed him by for improving his mind. Even while actually working in the factory he put a newly purchased book of Latin Grammar on the frame of the spinning jenny, and 'thus kept up a pretty constant study undisturbed by the roar of the machinery. To this part of my education I owe my present power of completely abstracting the mind from surrounding noises, so as to read and write with perfect comfort amidst the play of children or near the dancing and songs of savages.'

Always to the adult David Livingstone the Africans — for whom he sacrificed his life — were savages. And yet he loved them as much as man ever has.

But not all his youth was spent in the cotton factory. There were summer evenings and holidays, and then he loved to play about the burns and braes, collecting wild flowers, fossils — and fish. For the young Livingstone, soon to become a pillar of the Church, was an expert poacher, not averse to getting a salmon home by dangling it inside his brother Charlie's trousers as they walked, very close together, back to Shuttle Row.

But as a contemporary remarked, he had other interests: 'I didna think muckle o' that David Livingstone when he worked wi' me. He was aye lyin' on his belly readin' a book — '

A really Scottish devotion to knowledge, almost for its own sake, had seized him. By eighteen, promoted to spinner in the factory, he was using the wages to attend lectures in medicine and divinity. And, needless to say, he bought or borrowed every possible book on both subjects.

At the age of twenty, the call came. He applied to be a communicant member of the Independent Church at Hamilton. His father had held the office of deacon in that church for some years, having been gripped by religion while serving as a tea vendor. He also — for some reason known best to himself — altered the spelling of his age-old Scots name Livingston and added the final 'e'. The father cautiously left it to the kirk elders to decide his son's fitness or not for the honour, and these insisted on a study period of five months before the lad was considered a worthy entrant to that church.

Life is a chain of accidents — and it was the brand-new idea of medical missionaries that made the young man decide to go abroad. How very fortunate it was that he had elected to study both Medicine and Divinity, such normally disparate subjects!

But being a medical missionary required a wider knowledge than contained in those two subjects. He would need to know Greek (of all things) and Chemistry, and he would also need a far deeper knowledge of the other two than he already possessed.

Undaunted, he got his father's permission to study these subjects in Glasgow and moved into the only lodgings he could afford, for two shillings a week. The plan was that he would earn the money to keep himself in Glasgow by doing work at the Blantyre cotton factory during his vacations.

Somehow he did, and in the summer of 1838, when he was twenty-five, he was accepted by the London Missionary Society. He had chosen that body because it was the only completely non-sectarian one. He was sent for final studies to England, to London first, and then a parsonage in Essex — and here he very nearly failed to make the grade. His appearance, he learnt, was most unprepossessing, his manner uncouth. He had, furthermore, absolutely no ability to orate, to sermonize, from the pulpit.

This last charge was absolutely true. During the Essex training he was asked to deputize for a parson who had been taken ill. He was given adequate warning and he carefully prepared his sermon. But when the time came during the service for him to read out his text and then deliver some thoughts on the subject, he only just managed the text. After embarrassing seconds of total silence, he gulped and said, 'Friends, I have forgotten all I had to say'. A moment later he was out of the pulpit and heading for the door.

But somehow his real charm, his huge intelligence and his capacity for work won the day. He managed to keep well during these studies on a regular three hours' sleep each night and at last they passed him as fit in every way for overseas service as a missionary.

What was he like at the start of his career? Two colleagues can tell us a bit about him: 'He was middle-sized, firm upon his feet, light in the under-trunk, round and full in the chest. I have to admit he was not bonny. His face wore at all times the strongly marked lines of potent will —'.

The other found that: 'There was a truly indescribable charm about him which with all his ungainly ways and by no means winning face, attracted almost everyone.'

They say we have no control over the faces the good Lord gives us until we are forty. Then what is writ on them is entirely what we have written ourselves. And David Livingstone is a comically perfect example. Pictures taken of him in his thirties show a puzzled bigot's face half hidden behind its walrus moustache. Without doubt it is a 'by no means winning face'. But the pictures later in life show a face of compassion, understanding, quiet strength.

Missionaries were needed for Africa. His ambition had been to go to China, but as Britain was at war with that country this was impossible, and he agreed to be sent to the Dark Continent: 'I will go at once to Africa'. The London Missionary Society felt — with commendable insight — that he would be best suited to the task of opening up new ground, and that therefore he should not remain at a mission station.

While much of this was going on, Livingstone managed to take his medical degree in Glasgow, so that when he sailed in December, 1840, for Africa, he was as fully qualified as a man could want to be: a medical practitioner and ordained minister.

Halfway out, the sailing vessel *George* steered into a vicious storm, lost her foremast and had to limp across the South Atlantic to Rio de Janeiro for refit. Here he busied himself studying the Brazilian people, rather recklessly trying to convert a few of them to his own True Christianity. Yet he wrote home that the Roman Catholic Church in Brazil was beautiful and they really did things in style. 'If ever I join an Establishment it won't be either of the poor degenerate "sisters" at home, but the good mother herself in Brazil.' Yet, a few lines farther down we realize he was pulling our legs, for he adds earnestly, 'When will the beams of Divine Light dispel the darkness of the beautiful empire?'

Eventually — in March, 1841 — he arrived at Capetown. A few weeks later, after staying with a wise older man, Dr Philip, he and William Ross went on by ship to Port Elizabeth. Ross was a married man and in fact he and his wife had travelled out with Livingstone on the *George*. At Port Elizabeth the three of them waited another month for the ox-carts which would take them north to their destination, and during the month Livingstone pursued his study of both the Dutch and Sechuana languages.

The journey, when they eventually got their ox-carts, need not have taken ten weeks. But it did, largely because of the new medical missionary's determination to heal all *en route* who felt they needed it. But at the end of July, 1841, he reached the mission of Kuruman, in Bechuanaland, which had been established by Robert Moffat. It was a snug place — too snug, perhaps: smug, almost — and he admired its comfortable houses, its fine church, the forge, the carpenter's shop and so on. It had an air of prosperity and content- ment. But David Livingstone knew his role would be to press on, do his work much farther afield. Perhaps he irritated the inhabitants of the Kuruman mission by suggesting there were too many contented missionaries in residence and that they should be scattered miles apart. They should go out, one by one, and with what he called 'native agency' convert and succour the savages. Native agency, he felt, 'is the only thing that can evangelize the world'. He would stay only just long enough to master the Sechuana language and then go north to live 'excluded from all European society'.

And so began a lifetime serving Africa. He found that not only did the remote northern Africans need instruction more than those at hand, for they were totally ignorant, but that in fact there were far more of them. Kuruman mission seemed to have been dumped down in a remarkably underpopulated spot. He began making expeditions into the bush, spending a few days here, a week there, and sometimes recruiting an interested man to spread the Word among his own people.

But it was not until 1843 that he got permission to open a new station. By now the ceaseless double quest for knowledge and for willing recipients of what he himself had to offer, had made him into an explorer as well as a missionary. He began having his share of adventure, and quite early on was hideously savaged by a lion. The experience, coupled with his disappointment at the attitude of so many Africans towards his teaching, might have severely discouraged a lesser man, but not Livingstone. They asked him what he felt at the moment the lion leapt on him, and he said, in his dry way, 'I was wondering what part of me he'd eat first'.

Livingstone had always been a good shot, and would remain one: but from now on he would be unable to fire his gun from the right shoulder, would be forced to use the left, and sight with the left eye.

Perhaps it was the long convalescence following his near-fatal experience which warmed his heart towards the opposite sex. And perhaps the fact that he was an invalid had a similar effect upon the girl he was soon to marry. She was Robert Moffat's twenty-three-year-old daughter Mary, and now in 1844, when he himself was thirty-one, he married her.

Up to a point it was a successful marriage — though it has always seemed to me that David Livingstone should never have married at all. Certainly he approached the partnership with eyes unromantically open. His betrothed, he wrote to a friend, was 'not romantic, but a matter-of-fact lady, a little, thick, black-haired girl, sturdy and all I want'.

For this matter-of-fact little lady he built a house in his new, up-country mission of Mabotsa. His salary, as married man, was raised to £100 a year.

The work he and his wife did lives after them. Over his many years in Africa, Livingstone was to heal and, from time to time, convert Africans. Those he healed and helped in many, many ways must have run into hundreds of thousands. One of his greatest achievements — in the missionary sphere — was his exposure of the slave trade, which resulted in its abolition. But though it is as a selfless Christian that he left his mark on Africa, it is as the world's greatest explorer of modern times that he is remembered outside it.

The big journeys began in 1849. Some time previous he had made the acquaintance of the English explorer William Oswell (Mr Moffat had urged the explorer to press on another two hundred miles beyond Kuruman to Livingstone's mission and pick his son-in-law's brain), and in 1849 he joined him, and Mungo Murray, in a search for a great lake. No white man had ever seen it, but natives knew where it was. It was believed to be simply enormous, to stretch from horizon to horizon in all directions. Livingstone agreed to join the Englishmen: his knowledge of Africa would help them, and he would have the opportunity, with this well-equipped caravan, of opening up still more territory.

The journey was hazardous and unpleasant, but at last, on 1 August, 1849, they reached the enormous lake, Lake Ngami. He was excited by the discovery, but his chief interest remained in spreading the Word of God and healing the sick bodies of the Africans who now came up to him and asked his help. Already the great Livingstone's fame had preceded him, to a land no white man had ever seen. He busied himself getting his 'native agency' going in this unfamiliar part, getting others to learn a little religion, a little medicine, from him and go out to help their own people. To do this Livingstone had to learn yet another language, but he did so at speed.

The expedition made its way home and months later he was delighted to receive the Royal Geographical Society's award for discovering the lake. It was £25, and though he and Mary were very poor he blued the lot on a handsome watch for himself. As for the award, he wrote, tongue in cheek to his parents: 'It is from the Queen. You must be very loyal, all of you. Next time she comes your way, shout till you are hoarse.'

And where is Lake Ngami now? It has evaporated, vanished: it is a vast green plain. But Livingstone's mapping of the area and his route to it threw light on an absolutely unknown, unvisited part of Africa.

The next year Livingstone took Mary and the three small children north from their mission at Kolobeng, to show them his lake. (He noted that the level had already fallen three feet in the twelve months.) And now we come to see the one great fault in his character: he was quite unable and unwilling to see that his wife should not be subjected to this sort of hardship. His desire to have her with him, have her help him in his work as she did at the mission, completely over-ruled common humanity which would surely have insisted she stay at home.

Mary was pregnant with her fourth child, and she suffered greatly from the journey. She got back to Kolobeng in August, more dead than alive, and lost the child.

Livingstone in his journal wrote cheerfully: 'It was just as likely to have happened had we remained at home, and we have now one of our number in heaven.'

Mary's recovery was slow and only partial, and after — incredibly — an arduous trip with her husband to the Upper Zambezi during which she had another child, it became obvious even to her husband that she and the children must leave Africa, at least for a while. This personal matter, however, was overshadowed by Livingstone's great discovery that the Upper Zambezi River had been wrongly placed on the map — and by the fact that there were natives galore in this area who badly needed his help, and got it.

For Mary, who was a very brave girl, it was a terrible wrench to leave her husband and Africa; she loved them both very deeply. But she and the four children sailed from Capetown on 23 April, 1852.

Without his wife and children, the tale of Livingstone becomes more of a geography lesson. He went on, opening up the country, leaving his native assistants everywhere he could, to carry on his missionary work, and it was in 1855 that he made perhaps his greatest discovery.

He was following the great Zambezi to its mouth in Delagoa Bay, travelling in a light canoe, when suddenly he reached a small island. It was almost hidden in clouds of spray. He disembarked on it and then discovered that the island was projecting right out over a precipice. Over this a gigantic waterfall was tumbling, and he crawled to the very edge, lay down and watched in wonder. 'It had never been seen before by European eyes, but scenes so lovely must have been gazed on by angels in their flight.' He was always, throughout life, horrified by exaggeration and now he estimated the length of these falls as 'not less than six hundred yards'. They are, in fact, 1,900 yards in length, with a drop of up to 350 feet at the deeper end.

He named them after his queen, perhaps remembering his quip about 'shouting till you are hoarse' in her honour.

At the end of the next year he returned to England, to be acclaimed as the greatest explorer of the age, the man who had accomplished the most marvellous journey on record and necessitated the complete re-drawing of the map of Africa. All this was true.

Perhaps this was the finest hour of his life. For soon, owing to a difference of opinion with the London Missionary Society, he resigned from that body. When he set sail a second time for Africa it was with the appointment of Consul to Quelimane in Mozambique, near the mouth of the Zambezi. He was also in charge of an expedition with orders to explore east and central Africa.

This second visit to that continent was in many ways a failure, and the expedition, mismanaged by himself and beset by every sort of bad luck, was recalled. His wife, who had bravely and eagerly rejoined him in Africa, died in 1862 on a ship at the mouth of the Zambezi. The interminable delay in that fever-ridden spot — which caused her death — was largely the result of Livingstone's own total inability as an organizer. One of the ship's officers wrote, 'I have rarely seen a man so easily led as Dr Livingstone. I never saw such constant vacillations, blunders, delays and want of common thought and foresight.'

He was heartbroken at Mary's death, but still able to do valuable work. He now pointed out the horrors of slavery as practised by the Portuguese and was instrumental in stopping it. He found time to discover Lake Nyasa and lay the foundations of what would some day become Nyasaland. His name is still reverenced there, though Nyasaland's name has changed to Malawi.

He returned to Britain in July, 1864, and spent a whole year at home. His third and last visit to Africa began with the declared intention — sponsored by the Geographical Society — of discovering the sources of the Nile. He was completely lost to the world for five years, from 1866, and it was during these years that at last advancing years and the rigours of his life began to take their toll. Disasters followed each other: his goods were stolen, his medicines lost, he nearly died half a dozen times from disease or starvation. And it was at his lowest ebb that he was found by Henry Stanley, sent by the go-ahead editor of the *New York Herald*.

Stanley was in almost every way the antithesis of Livingstone. He was brash and boastful. But the two men conceived a great respect for each other. Their friendship began, as everyone knows, when Stanley got to Ujiji and saw this walking skeleton, 'pale and wearied, with a grey beard, wearing a blueish cap with a faded gold band round it, a red-sleeved waistcoat and a pair of grey tweed trousers'. Stanley's first words were: 'Doctor Livingstone, I presume?'

The two men stayed together till March, 1872, exploring still more of Africa, until Stanley reluctantly had to go home. He urged the explorer to come with him, but Livingstone refused: now, with Mary dead, the continent was more than ever his life, his work. Ill with malaria and dysentery, he set off again for the sources of the Nile which he fancied were near yet another lake he had discovered, Bangweulu.

He never got there. In April, 1863, he scribbled in his journal, 'Tried to ride, but was forced to lie down, and they carried me back to the village exhausted'.

It was the end. When he reached the village — Chitambo — his grief-stricken attendants built him a hut, and there he died.

And now these devoted Africans, who could easily have left the body where it lay, endured the most dreadful hardships, including battle and bloodshed, to get it to the coast. There it was taken by ship to England and a hero's burial in Westminster Abbey.

Perhaps we can sum up David Livingstone and his life, with its selflessness and yet complete lack of consideration for people — like Mary — whom he did not understand; its fantastic courage and complete lack of organizing ability; with his words:

'I am a missionary, heart and soul. God had an only Son, and He was a missionary and a physician. A poor, poor imitation I am or wish to be. In this service I hope to live, in it, I wish to die.'

But no — we cannot leave him as just a saint. He was not a saint:
he was a good, yet sometimes selfish man. He even had a sense of
humour — at the expense of the ladies:

'I notice that the mongoose gets lean on a diet of cockroaches.
That would be invaluable to fat young ladies at home —'.

Andrew Carnegie

He embodied much that is fine in the Scots character — and quite a bit which is not. He was an economic wizard, persuasive, charming and fantastically hard-working. When it suited him, he was fantastically generous. He had the common touch, so that even when he was many times a millionaire and exploiting his workmen, they would do whatever he told them — so long as he told it personally. They would rise in revolt against an unpleasant order, if it were handed down by an underling.

He was embittered, childishly embittered, against all those born with the proverbial silver spoon in the mouth, and this included all royalty, all aristocracy. He was boastful; the science of Public Relations, Image Building, which was unknown in his day, might have been thought up by Andrew Carnegie. Other rich men might have retrospective qualms about the way they made their money.

Never Carnegie. We may compare him with John D. Rockefeller, who made more money and gave more away.

To do so, let us creep aboard an ocean liner which is just about to sail from New York. Gangways are being removed, gongs are sounding, there is an atmosphere of noise and excitement. Yet down below in his cabin sits Mr Rockefeller, with the door locked. He is deeply ashamed of the money he possesses, conscious that there has been a deal of unpleasantness recently about the way he is alleged to have made it. He has crept aboard under an assumed name and slunk down to his cabin. He may well not leave it throughout the seven-day journey to Europe.

Above his head — some four decks above it — stands Andrew Carnegie, four years his senior and another multi-millionaire about whom unpleasant questions have been asked. But the round-faced, jolly Scot is the man everyone loves, and the press is clustered round him like bees at a honey-pot, busily scribbling down his views, his opinions, on philosophy, the world situation, and himself. By tomorrow morning half the newspapers in the world will have columns about the great philanthropist.

There will be nothing about the grasping Rockefeller.

And we must admit that Andrew Carnegie, ruthless maker of money, inexhaustible giver-away, is a more interesting character than John Rockefeller, who was both these things, only more so. For that he can thank the fact that he was born in Scotland.

The event took place in a cottage at Dunfermline. The year was 1835. Like the cottages in which so many of our famous men and women were born, it contained a hand-loom, and on it Thomas Carnegie made table-cloths.

His hard-working wife, Margaret, who will figure throughout much of the Carnegie story, made shoes and sold them in her own little shop to supplement Thomas's earnings. She also ruled the family with an iron hand.

A predilection for revolt has long been a Scots characteristic, and the Carnegies were no exception. They quarrelled with their church, their neighbours, the local laird. In this they were surpassed only by Margaret Carnegie's family, the Morrisons, who got so acrimoniously involved with the Laird of Pittencrieff that he swore no one of Morrison blood should ever enter his grounds. Young Andrew took this to heart and immediately became a rabid hater of all lairds. The hate, as life wore on, would extend to royalty.

His mother, staunch, determined woman with a mind of her own, kept his thoughts in this direction. Her control over her son till he was an elderly man is one of the oddest facets of an odd career.

Years before, a member of the family had emigated to America and settled in Pennsylvania. Now, with their fortunes low, the Carnegies decided to follow. It was 1848; Andrew was thirteen, his brother Tom just five. They packed their few belongings, said goodbye to their neighbours and set off across Scotland to Glasgow. Here they embarked and sailed west.

Once across the Atlantic they moved inland to settle near Uncle Willie in the township of Allegheny, in Pennsylvania. It was a primitive place, unconnected by rail to anywhere and supplied only by river steamer up the Monongahela River. Thomas and Margaret Carnegie were discouraged, for the place seemed even less promising than Dunfermline. Young Andrew found his first weeks, working in a cotton mill, thoroughly depressing; but he kept eyes and ears open and within a month of arrival had transferred to the Telegraph Company as messenger boy.

The job only involved carrying telegrams from the receiving station to the addressee, but he set himself to work learning the Morse code. Soon, like other young and ambitious telegraphists of the period, he was able to listen to the clickerty-clack of the sounder and read off whole sentences out loud, without putting pencil to paper. This was Thomas Edison's proudest achievement as a young man and, at the time, it was wee Andrew Carnegie's.

For he *was* wee. A wee blond mannie with a round face and large eyes. Not Rockefeller eyes that stared through one, but round, innocent, visionary orbs that seemed to be looking at something far off, in the future.

Or in the past. Andrew Carnegie built his life, as soon as he was rich enough, round the memory of Scotland. As luck would have it — for luck, as with all of us, good luck and bad, makes a difference — he was rich enough remarkably soon.

His father died and he was now alone with his canny, doting

mother, and young Tom; the responsibility determined him to be more than just the best telegraphist in Pennsylvania. He remembered the land from which he had sprung, made up his mind to be a worthy descendant. As he wrote later, 'Every Scotchman is two Scotchmen, as his land has the wild barren stern crags and mountain peaks, and also the smiling valleys where the mildest foxglove and bluebell blossom, so the Scotchman with his rugged force and hard intellect has a heart capable of being touched to the finest issue.'

The luck? Ah, yes. The railway, when it reached Pittsburgh, was one of the wonders of the world, and its arrival coincided with the maturity of a boy who had become not only a superb telegraphist, but the most promising man in the neighbourhood. The new Superintendent of the Pennsylvania Railroad in Pittsburgh signed the boy up as his personal assistant and sent him off, for a start, in charge of gangs of men repairing the track, track which in those early days needed constant attention.

Then, one day, there was a nasty train crash. It coincided (luck again here) with the absence on business of Mr Scott and brought about total confusion. The line had been blocked and no one knew how to disentangle the mess. One after another, goods trains were coming to a halt all over Pennsylvania.

The young assistant took charge instantly. He sent telegrams to each train, giving the driver an exact time to move off, and signing each message 'Thomas A. Scott'. Such a method of telegraph control had been tried, but no one yet understood it. Under Andrew Carnegie it worked beautifully; the railroad paralysis ended and the Pennsylvania got back on the move.

Thomas A. Scott, when he got back to Pittsburgh, could only gasp at the success obtained by his white-haired Scotch devil.

The Scotch devil had become, overnight, a man to be reckoned with. And now, another stroke of luck. A mysterious stranger walked in, carrying an ingenious wooden model which turned out to be a folding bed, suitable for putting inside a rail carriage. By day the carriage would be comfortable, seated; at night it converted easily into a honeycomb of little private alcoves for sleeping. Carnegie persuaded his firm that this would be the design of railway carriages in the future, and they not only agreed to manufacture them, but formed a separate company to build them *en masse*. Young Andrew, having discovered the design, was allowed to be majority shareholder. By this time a gifted carpenter had been found to supervise the manufacture of these cars, and he added his own improvements. His name was George Pullman.

And now, somehow, Andrew Carnegie found himself the new Superintendent of the Pittsburgh Division, Pennsylvania Railroad. Thomas A. Scott faded from the picture.

With inside information about where the Railroad would go and when, Carnegie got into the lucrative habit of buying the right stocks and shares cheaply in the knowledge that they would soon be worth a great deal more. His wealth grew every month, and well before he was thirty he found himself a millionaire. Under the eagle eye of his mother, every penny was carefully reinvested.

Came the American Civil War and he was able to give valuable assistance to the northern side by his handling of the railways. Tracks and bridges were kept in first-class repair and troop-trains were slotted in, one after the other, with a skill that puzzled and delighted the military authorities.

And then, at the end of the war, this rich young man took a trip back home to Scotland — and he realized that his heart belonged there. His aunt in Dunfermline, delighted to see that the lad had made a bit of money, suggested kindly that he open up a wee shoppie in the town of his ancestors. He smilingly declined.

Back in Pittsburgh, he took stock and pondered the question of culture. He had always read copiously; now he set himself to doing it like a military exercise. The whole of Shakespeare was consumed within weeks, much of it committed to memory. He joined a debating society, met men more sophisticated than himself and studied them, their behaviour, what made them tick.

He was invited to one of their houses, far grander than his own, and there in the library he saw words carved over the fireplace which he committed to memory on the spot. He would remember them for the rest of his life:

> He that cannot reason is a fool,
> He that will not reason is a bigot;
> He that dare not reason is a slave.

He swapped heavy boots for a gentleman's shoes, mastered the art of small talk, became much in demand in Pittsburgh society. Girls who had once fought shy of the ponderous little man now found him attractive, wondered why their interest was not returned. They had forgotten Margaret Carnegie.

As a millionaire, Andrew had no need to remain an employee of the Pennsylvania Railroad, and he resigned. He invested in iron and in a new device called a trip-hammer which shaped pig-iron more simply and effectively than any other method. The inventor, a man called Kloman, had no business acumen and soon Carnegie and his mother were partners in his enterprise.

The Kloman firm, now with all these limitless funds behind it, was set for a prosperous future. And then one day, Kloman, never quite sure what hit him, was out in the street.

From iron, by easy and obvious stages, to bridges. The Carnegie-financed Keystone Bridge Company crossed the Ohio at Cincinnati, the Missouri at Plattsmouth, the Mississippi at St Louis. And with new bridges, new lines were opened; the rails for them were made by another Carnegie enterprise, the Union Iron Works. The middle west had begun shouting for everything the east could send it, and demanding railways to transport it; Carnegie made it his job to see they got them.

Young Tom now got married and Andrew moved with his mother to New York, to a hotel off Broadway. He had discovered that his talent lay in persuading others to do what he wanted; this he could do more comfortably, more effectively, from New York, while leaving the humdrum work of building bridges, making rails, to subordinates.

He realized suddenly that if he never worked again he would still have a tax-free income of fifty thousand dollars a year. At the same time he realized the difficulty of spending such an amount on himself and his mother.

He would leave America immediately, go to Britain and study at Oxford. There he would get a degree — and he would have been educated. The feeling of inferiority which crept up on him in the company of people with culture would vanish.

On second thought, it could wait. He would go to Oxford in two years' time.

The lure of profit intervened. And to be fair to Carnegie, we must add that it was not simply the glitter of gold; it was the shimmer of steel. On a visit to England he had been to a factory where the new Bessemer converter, for making pig-iron cheaply and efficiently into steel, was being used. It was a revelation; the molten pig-iron was brought to white heat simply by bubbling air through it, without any further addition of heat. And then, with air cut off at a predetermined point — a white and bubbling liquid which was steel. Childishly, magically simple; it would revolutionize the nineteenth century, change the world of iron into a world of steel.

Henry Bessemer, the cheerful English wizard who invented more things than Baird, and far more profitably, was allowing this particular brainchild to be operated anywhere under licence, for a very reasonable figure. Carnegie was genuinely fascinated by the process and he now plunged into the steel business as if it were the only thing in life that mattered. His young brother Tom had an option on a site called Braddock by the Monongahela River which would be ideal for a Carnegie steelworks. Andrew made haste to take the option up.

In his autobiography he wrote that an inspiration came to him in bed, telling him this great new enterprise would be sited at a place to be called Braddock.

You may take your choice.

He built his steelworks where Tom and the Lord told him. And now we get a glimpse of the sort of insight which really made Carnegie rich and great. He learnt that another steelworks, not far off, was on strike, that the leader of the strikers was a man called Bill Jones, whom the men would follow whatever he asked them to do. Carnegie signed him up immediately and put him in charge of his own labour relations. Bill Jones might have his troubles today, but in nineteenth-century Pennsylvania he worked wonders. The men, at his suggestion, were paid very high wages and divided into teams which competed against each other in productivity. (The very thought makes a late-twentieth-century mind reel.) At the end of the day the furnace which had produced the most was allowed to hoist a flag and keep it aloft for twenty-four hours, egging on others to get it pulled down. It was made clear, too, that any man good enough could become a boss. As for Bill Jones — Captain Bill, as he was universally known — he refused Carnegie's offer of a partnership and settled simply for the role of 'the highest-paid working man in the United States of America'. At 25,000 dollars a year he was.

Carnegie came to a friendly agreement with the railways about transporting his steel, much the same arrangement that Rockefeller had reached about oil: cheap transport meant cheap steel for the railway, and it also in effect meant no transport for anyone else's steel. Such action today would be illegal, but in the forceful nineteenth century it was accepted business practice; no sort of bribe or blackmail was considered out of order.

By 1880 the Carnegie steel interests were producing more steel than any firm had ever done, and their steel was being rushed about the USA, at cut rates, to build bridges, and to lay down rails on which to carry more steel. And, of course, to carry the wonderful Pullman car, which Carnegie owned.

He certainly didn't need any more money. But now it was exciting, and there could be no question of swapping the world of steel for Oxford. What he would do, and did do, from 1880 onwards, was spend half of each year in Europe. For the first of these European visits he took a party of friends in a stage-coach. He wrote the exploit up in a little book called *An American Four-in-Hand in Britain*, and the writing of this, his first book, seems to have meant as much to him as any of the take-overs, the successes, of the past. 'To do things,' he now proclaimed, 'is not half the battle. Carlyle is all wrong about this. To be able to tell the world what you have done, that is the greater accomplishment.'

Hence, we might almost say, Public Relations.

He bought up a prettily named rival steelworks, Homestead, a few miles away. Homestead had suffered a lot of labour troubles and Carnegie watched till these were at their very worst and made a very low bid — which was thankfully accepted. He put in a manager, Henry Frick, and retired for six months to Scotland.

And in his absence a strike far worse than those which had afflicted Homestead in the old days descended over the whole of Carnegie Steel. A union had been formed, The Amalgamated Association, and it demanded better conditions. Earnings on piece-work could be very high, but men worked a twelve-hour shift and sometimes a non-stop twenty-four. This, Amalgamated said, just wasn't good enough.

The first threat of a strike met strong-arm tactics from Frick; to prevent victimization of men who stayed at work, he took the fantastic step of ordering three hundred men from the Pinkerton Detective Agency in New York — virtually a private army.

News of this got out, and when a tug came up the Monongahela drawing behind it two barges full of Pinkertons and crates of rifles, a barrage of small-arms fire greeted it from the shore.

Panic on board, for the rifles were still in their crates. And a knotty legal problem to solve — with bullets whistling past: the local Sheriff was on board, and he had been expected to give a straightforward blessing to the Pinkerton invasion, but he did not. Each man would have to be individually sworn in as Sheriff's Assistant. Furthermore, this could not be done until they were on dry land. The cursing Pinkertons lay flat on the deck while bullets screamed overhead.

The tug cast them adrift, beat a hasty retreat. The strikers poured burning oil on the river. The Pinkertons slowly unpicked the crates — from their horizontal position — and prepared to do battle.

But they were forced to surrender; and although the strike leader gave them safe conduct to get ashore and escape, the unfortunate Pinkertons were attacked with stones and broken bottles.

This was civil war: and unlike the one of a generation previous, it was devoid of profit for Carnegie. The massacre became a national scandal. Carnegie, who had been sending contradictory orders from Scotland, where he was fishing salmon, rushed back and settled the affair. It is an indication of the man's charm, his common touch, that whereas his manager Frick, who had done most of what he did because Carnegie either suggested it or acquiesced, was nearly murdered by the men, one of them said to Carnegie, 'The men would have let you trick them — but they wouldn't let that other man stroke their hair."

Whether this influenced the next, astonishing stage in Carnegie's career — the chief one we remember — one cannot say. He became a philanthropist. He had acquired an education from his own reading; he would now offer that same opportunity to all the world. He gave a magnificent library to Allegheny, another to Pittsburgh. He announced that *any community in the English-speaking world* might have a library, but it would have to prove to Andrew Carnegie that it intended to stock it with books and set aside a reasonable sum each year for upkeep.

Libraries sprang up in Britain and America — and with them art galleries, technical colleges.

He took time off to write another book. This was a very odd book, setting out to prove that because Andrew Carnegie was an ordinary man, only ordinary men were capable of achieving greatness. Only ordinary men could discover minerals, build railways, plan cities. The book was called *Triumphant Democracy* and it asserted that republicanism was the answer to the world's ills; that no nation could prosper under a monarchy or an aristocracy.

It is a strange twenty-four chapters' worth of egotism: an ode to materialism. America, he points out, is OK because she has avoided the Frenchy corruption of Europe. A union between America and Britain would be a good thing, but impossible of achievement while Britain hangs on to its outmoded monarchy: the monarchy must go. The aristocracy must go.

And up in Carnegie's great Scottish home, his castle of Skibo in Sutherland, where some of this has been written, the most honoured guests are from the British peerage.

Margaret Carnegie died when her son was in his fifties. Tom had died some years before that. Only now did Andrew Carnegie feel himself free to marry. He was over sixty when his daughter was born.

And now, at last, the great man, with a little girl playing about his feet at Skibo, had become a human being. The philanthropy, of course, had started years before, but it went on now, redoubled. He went on with his giving of libraries (and the total spent on this alone soon reached £10,000,000) and now he gave £2,000,000 for Scottish education. This was followed up by vast sums to American and English universities. For his old home of Dunfermline he set up a trust with an annual income of £25,000.

In 1904 he hit upon the imaginative idea of a Carnegie Hero Fund. At first it was for the USA and Canada, but it was extended to cover Britain as well, by 1908. Its laudable purpose was 'to place those following peaceful vocations who have been injured in an heroic effort to save human life in somewhat better positions pecuniarily than before, until again able to work'.

Carnegie Trusts, Carnegie Foundations, Carnegie Endowments, poured out money, all of it for excellent causes — more money than most small nations earned over the same period. There was the Carnegie Foundation for the Advancement of Teaching, the Carnegie Endowment for International Peace, the Carnegie Trust for Universities of Scotland, the Carnegie United Kingdom Trust . . .

Till the end of life he would spend spring and summer in Europe — most of it at Skibo, where that representative of effete monarchy, Edward VII, was an honoured guest — and the autumn and winter in America. As time ran out and age crept up, Carnegie's attempts to do something really worthwhile with his money grew ever greater. He disbelieved in churches, but he liked hymns — and the number of church organs he gave in the last years of his life rose into the hundreds.

He died, universally mourned, at the age of eighty-four, having given away some 300 million dollars. Here, men knew, was a man, a real man like themselves, who had been doing just the sort of thing they would have done themselves, had they been in similar circumstance.

Here, in fact, was a man no better and no worse than any other: a man like one or two others who had made a fortune and gave a lot of it back again. But the larger-than-life image of that man, putting paid to heresies about Scotsmen being tight-fisted with their bawbees — this has ensured that the name of Andrew Carnegie will be remembered, with gratitude, till the end of time.

Alexander Graham Bell

There's a saying to the effect that 'a man above the common herd will have a son as far beneath'. Or words to that effect. Like most axioms it overstates its case and usually isn't true.

But lots of remarkable men do have completely unremarkable children. Or remarkably awful ones.

Yet I wonder how many families have axed the axiom as thoroughly as the family Bell? Adding a bit more lustre each time, through two more generations?

Our subject is the last of the Bells (there were no more after the famous one, who liked to sign himself 'A.G.B.') which gives a rather pompous garnish to the life of a delightful, multi-talented and witty man. But to understand the inventor of the telephone one has to understand the Bell family.

Our story begins with 'A.G.B.''s grandfather, a simple maker of shoes, a cobbler who was born in 1790 and brought up in St Andrews, on the Fife coast. As far back as he could remember, his forebears had been cobblers, and good ones. He was proud of his calling and might happily have spent a whole working life at it.

One feels rather like a schoolmaster saying, 'Now sit up and pay attention'. But a warning has to be given at this stage that all three Bells we are discussing were christened Alexander. One resists the temptation to style them Alex I, Alex II and Alex III.

For cobbler Alex, marriage in 1814 to the stage-struck Elisabeth Colville was to change everything. He found himself slithering into amateur dramatics — and this was to alter not only his life, but that of his descendants.

And the world.

Acting became an obsession and, soon, a way of life. He loved it and found he could earn a little money by it — not in sleepy St Andrews, but in the city of Edinburgh, where he went with Elisabeth, abandoning his cobbler's last to join her on the stage. He found he had a natural histrionic gift, a sense of humour and, above all, a beautifully articulated voice. He was described in an Edinburgh journal as 'a highly amusing actor, with his numerous roles spoken in the Scottish dialect.'

But cobbler Alex wasn't content with just 'a Scottish dialect': he quickly taught himself to speak in any dialect he chose, including what we now call southern standard English. He began to study the science of voice production and soon found he was making more money, deriving more satisfaction, from giving elocution lessons.

Their stage work had given Bell and his wife a hobby but little more, and they'd had to run an Edinburgh tavern to make ends meet. Now a new avenue had opened up, and with the same impetuosity which had taken him from St Andrews, Alex and Elisabeth left for Dundee to start a school of elocution. They had rightly surmised that this flourishing, expanding, town would have a population of self-made men and women who wanted their children to grow up speaking well.

They prospered — for nine years. Then, in a situation more relevant to 20th-Century soap opera than life in the 19th, the Scottish career was over. Bell's wife had an affair with the rector of

Dundee Academy which lasted so long before the preoccupied Bell
even noticed, that he was forced to sue for divorce, which he was
granted.

Then his wife's devoted servant girl decided to wreak vengeance
by claiming her own illegitimate child to be his.

There seems not a shred of evidence to support this claim, but
the wealthy burghers of Dundee were suitably shocked and with-
drew their offspring, in shoals, from Bell's school. Nothing
daunted, he travelled south to London, where his fame had preceded him. He took with him his son Alex Melville Bell, who at 13
was already showing an interest in the art of voice production. The
other two children of the marriage stayed with their mother.

Bell senior prospered in London and started devoting more of his
time to scientific analysis and less to teaching. He published 'The
Practical Elocutionist', with symbols representing vocal sounds,
their emphasis and their grouping.

But he had one great worry: the health of his son Melville. The
boy had never been well and the dampness of London seemed to
make him worse. At last, in 1838, when Melville was 19, he was
shipped off to St Johns, Newfoundland, to stay with a friend of the
Bells who'd emigrated.

He made an astonishing recovery and soon was able to hold down
a job as clerk in a shipping firm, while carrying on the family
tradition and giving lessons in speech.

And it was here, in the New World, that a bold idea struck.
Elocution was not to be a crutch for social climbers and aspiring
actors: it would be a life-line for people with real speech impedi-
ments. Most important of all — it would teach deaf people, who'd
never heard a human voice, how to speak.

Melville made a huge success of it, basing his work firmly on old
Alex's development of 'visual sounds' in his handbook. And the
link between father and son was so close, and real, that the cured
and healthy Melville left Newfoundland after four years to rejoin
the one-time cobbler, in London, as a partner. Old Alex was now a
Professor of Elocution and he looked forward to a long and fruitful
partnership.

It lasted exactly a year. Twenty-five-year-old Melville paid a visit

to Edinburgh, met a beautiful — and partly deaf — girl, Eliza Grace
Symonds, and married her. He was enchanted by the Scottish
capital which he'd left a dozen years before as semi-invalid, and as
Eliza preferred it to the unknown south, he decided to stay. He was
working on a book, 'The Art of Reading', and Edinburgh was a
congenial place to work.

So — not before time, you say — we have the subject of this
article, the man who invented the telephone, being born of Melville
and Eliza Bell, in Edinburgh. The date is 3 March 1847.

But don't think that Melville's role, or even that of old Alex, is
over. Far from it. The joys of matrimony blinded Melville to the
memory of his own sickly childhood. Of the three fine boys Eliza
bore him, only one survived to full maturity. His name — yes —
was Alexander Bell, without even a middle initial. He adopted that
himself on his 11th birthday — the surname of a Canadian boy who
was staying with them. No doubt in later years the adult Mr Graham
felt proud of all the ingenious things to which his name had been
attached. 'A.G.B.' had metamorphosed from plain Alex Bell, on an
11th birthday.

The lives of all three Bell generations were full of activity and
achievement within the United Kingdom right up until 1870 when
Melville — at last — decided to take his one surviving, sickly son
back to the Canada which had saved his own life. We can spare little
time for those years except for the remarkable feats performed by
the three youngest Bells — A.G.B., or 'Aleck'; Melly; and Ted in
their teens — of whom two would not survive.

Melville, their father, had perfected old Alex's Visible Speech: a
phonetic alphabet of great accuracy and complexity. He would get
a group of friends to recite poems in strange dialects, read bits from
the paper in funny voices, even sing songs. The three boys (who'd
been kept well away from all this) were then invited in and given the
script their father had been making of the performance. Without a
moment's hesitation they were into their act. Exactly as the
originators had said them, the words came out. Comical foreign
accents, a few bars of a Welsh folk tune, newspaper stories read in
'braid Scots' and 'posh English', were all faithfully rendered — to
the astonishment of those who'd perpetrated them.

The only other happening we need log is that old Alex (the cobbler/Professor) asked plaintively if his 15-year-old grandson, Aleck (as he liked to be called, and spelled, even after the adding of a middle initial) might join him in London. After all, the boy's father had come back from Canada for just that purpose, and then abandoned it for Edinburgh. And we log it simply because Aleck Graham Bell was to describe it as 'the turning point in my life. It converted me from a boy somewhat prematurely into a man, at fifteen'.

That boy's two brothers died, his grandfather died, and as the lad Melly was being lowered into his grave, next to his brother Ted and his grandfather Alex, in Highgate Cemetery, London, Aleck's father knew he had no choice. Back to Canada, just as he himself had gone, forty two years before.

This time it would be for ever.

So the 23-year-old Alexander Graham Bell, elocutionist, expert in Visual Speech and already a small-time inventor (a 'wheat cleaner' and an 'artificial larynx', neither of which got far beyond the drawing board) arrived with his father and mother at Brantford, Ontario, in August 1870.

The family's fame had preceded them and Aleck's father, Melville, was offered a professorship over the border, in Boston, Massachusetts. He preferred to carry on with his scientific work and it was agreed that young Aleck would take the job — when his health permitted.

Aleck made a success of the job, but like his father Melville, he found his mind seething with ideas. Ideas which needed money, as well as freedom from the time-table of lectures, demonstrations and therapy. He resigned his post, managing to make ends meet by fitting private, fee-paying pupils into his life.

And it was during this period that he found himself experimenting with a brand new idea.

This, though it seemed unlikely to be of help to the deaf, had entered his mind through experiments with the human voice. Now, though his work with the deaf would go on undiminished, there seemed a chance of making a great deal of money. And, for the first time in his life, Aleck Bell wanted money. He was in love.

In love with the daughter of a wise and influential businessman, Gardiner Greene Hubbard. His daughter Mabel was beautiful, intelligent and just 16.

She was also totally deaf which is how she had come to Aleck's attention. Her father turned to him for help and advice.

Suddenly everything was happening at once. He'd just been appointed (at a salary hardly commensurate with the awesome title) Professor of Vocal Physiology and Elocution at Boston University. He was in love with Mabel Hubbard and overjoyed at being asked to take her on as a private pupil. (He would cheerfully have done this for love alone, but Hubbard ensured that he was well rewarded.) And he simultaneously grew obsessed with the money-making idea of a Multiple Telegraph — which would give him the funds to ask for the girl's hand in marriage.

The theory behind the device was closely allied to Aleck's study of the human voice and ear. If he could make it work, one pair of wires would send far more than one message at a time. The principle was of 'tuning' a telegraph receiver to its distant transmitter, by sending the dots and dashes of the Morse Code in buzzes of different pitch. If each receiver only responded to the pitch at which it was set, he'd be successful.

The idea met with approval from Gardiner Greene Hubbard (who had not yet been approached about Aleck's designs on his daughter) and he gave it every encouragement. As a businessman, he saw its financial implications, and as a friend of the younger man, was anxious that he should have a great success — which the Multiple Telegraph gave every sign of producing.

But progress was slow and frustrating. Aleck had acquired a young assistant, a country boy from a livery stable in Salem, by name, Thomas Watson, and when time and opportunity permitted they experimented far into the night with the telegraph. Sometimes they seemed to have the problem solved. Then, a minute later, none of the metal reeds they were using to tune transmitter with receiver would respond to its partner. A message coming through clearly on one receiver would suddenly either transfer its affections to another, or cut off altogether.

They found that an angry shout into the assembly of reeds at one end would give a faint echo at the receiving lot. At first, this seemed of little significance, as a 'blast!' a 'damn!' or a 'curse it!' came through exactly like any other expletive — just a sad, sympathetic, hum.

Then Bell's fertile imagination hit on the idea of tinkering with the device to see if a pair of wires could be made to transmit recogniseable words, a voice down the wire.

Tom Watson shared his enthusiasm immediately, and the two young men grew hoarse, shouting into various adaptations of their transmitter with its differently tuned reeds, and getting a faint, meaningless buzz at the far end.

Work on the Multiple Telegraph was inevitably held up and this caused great annoyance to Gardiner Hubbard. Aleck, having found that Mabel returned his affection, had waited until she was 17 and then asked her hand in marriage. The Hubbard family, believing their future son-in-law to be a hard-working, level-headed man destined for fame and fortune, agreed. Now, they were no longer amused. Unless Aleck gave up this time-wasting nonsense of electric speech (*what* an absurd idea!) and concentrated on his telegraph, he must abandon hope of marrying Mabel.

And so we come to those words which have gone down in history like 'Dr Livingstone, I presume?', 'England expects every man ...' and so on. On 10 March 1876, after months in which there'd been no noticeable progress since the first feeble echo of an angry inventor's voice (albeit an electric one) — it happened. The faithful Tom was listening, ear hard against the Bell's receiver, for anything that might come through from the next room. They'd adjusted both machines a dozen times during the morning. Suddenly — perfectly, frighteningly, clear — came the words:

'Mr Watson, come here — I want you!'

(For years legend had it that Aleck Bell had spilt a flask of acid down his clothes and was calling, as he thought, through a doorway for help. But this has now been dismissed as folk-lore. Bell never mentioned acid in any of his writings — and in any case, how could Tom Watson be of much help? We owe the story to Watson himself, who produced the fanciful anecdote fifty years later, in his own autobiography.)

We do know that Tom Watson heard his own name, loud and clear, coming over the wires. Whether or not he'd been summoned, he tore into the next room and blurted out the news.

Like children playing a game, a vocal musical chairs, the pair of them hopped from one room to the other, reciting poems to each other, singing snatches of song.

At last, the first words had travelled by wire. That night Aleck wrote to his mother, 'March 10th 1876 — this is a great day for me. I feel that I have at last struck the solution of a great problem and the day is coming when telegraph wires will be laid on to houses just like water or gas, and friends converse with each other without leaving home.'

'Telegraph wires'. The word telephone hadn't yet been coined — nor would it be for many years.

His prospective father-in-law, Mr Hubbard, was given a demonstration of this speech by wire, and, amazingly, was quite unimpressed, still insisting that Aleck perfect his Multiple Telegraph. And it was this (which still had many imperfections and lacked reliability) which Hubbard arranged for Aleck to demonstrate at the United States Centennial Exhibition a little later in the year, rather than 'the voice down the wire' (which was more perfect than its inventor had dreamed it could be — and worked every time).

But Aleck was nobody's fool. The Multiple Telegraph was demonstrated, with considerable success and to considerable applause. Then, before the various dignitaries could escape, he asked diffidently if they would like to see 'an invention in embryo', the transmission of speech down a pair of wires.

Sir William Thomson, later to be Lord Kelvin, was one of those who politely agreed to witness the young man's demonstration of something which was obviously absurd fantasy.

There was a courteous, if rather restless, silence, and then suddenly a voice emerged loud and clear from a little box on a table, singing 'God Save The Queen'.

Absolutely stunned, the audience looked around them for Mr Bell, then realised that he had absented himself several minutes before — and that this voice from the box was his!

The inventor then delivered a few words of greeting, followed by the question, 'Do you understand what I say?'

'Yes — yes, I do!' shouted Thomson, almost knocking over Pedro II, the Emperor of Brazil, in a mad rush to the stage. When Bell appeared from an adjoining room, Thomson shook him by the hand. 'This,' he said, 'is the most marvellous thing I have seen in America!' A visiting Japanese, Mr Issawa, asked whether the machine spoke Japanese as well, and was delighted to be shown it did.

This first publicly demonstrated telephone consisted of an electromagnet with an armature connected to a flexible diaphragm, and the device served as both transmitter and receiver. The vibrations of the thin diaphragm in response to vibrations of the human voice caused a fluctuating current in the coils of the electromagnet. This current could be made to affect the electromagnet at the receiver, so its diaphragm vibrated exactly in sympathy with the transmitter's. A battery in circuit improved reception over a distance, but as the device was both transmitter and receiver, having to be moved from mouth to ear, it was awkward for normal conversation.

Awkward or not, it was a thumping great success, and Mr Hubbard was happy to agree that the Multiple Telegraph could wait. Mr A.G. Bell had more than proved his suitability as a husband for Mabel.

The marriage took place on 11 July 1877. And it was such a long and happy one that it is easy to forget that Mabel Hubbard was, and would remain, totally deaf. (For that matter, Aleck's mother was almost stone deaf. It would be very unfair to suggest that father and son married girls upon whom they could practise their methods of communication, but the deafness of both wives does seem more than a coincidence.)

A brief honeymoon in Boston and Ontario was followed by embarkation for Britain. And the inventor's signature, when he used it, changed this year from Aleck, which Mabel seems to have found clumsy and affected, to plain Alec. Which simply made the man himself use the initials A.G.B. all the more — and be grateful that he'd adopted the middle name 'Graham' at the age of 11. 'A.B.' would have been most unimpressive.

What was he like — this Alexander Graham Bell?

Large, black-bearded, with a glorious voice, great skill as singer and pianist, and an enormous sense of fun. He also had a tendency to put on weight. In September 1877, when their U.K. trip had taken them to his native Scotland, Mabel wrote his mother: 'Last night Alec swallowed a whole dish of finnan haddock which was intended for us both. In fact, he is growing tremendously stout and can hardly get his wedding trousers on now.' (Between his July wedding and October of the same year his weight climbed from 165 to 201 lbs.)

He was interested in almost everything and at the time of Mabel's letter from Aberdeen was already studying the flight of seagulls and planning a flying machine. Later, in Canada, he was to make one which *almost* flew, and there seems little doubt that if he hadn't had so many ideas fizzing through his mind at once, it would have. One brilliant idea (which was to be upstaged by Marconi's development of radio communication) was talking along a beam of light. Instead of a pair of wires, Bell used the fluctuating intensity of light aimed at a primitive photo-electric cell — a test-tube of the element selenium which alters its electrical resistance when light falls on it. The 'Doctor Livingstone' remark associated with this particular discovery has always fascinated me with its happy mixture of the music hall and laboratory: 'Mr Bell, if you hear what I say, come to the window and wave your hat!'

What a picture it conjures up! But Mr Bell, four years after his invention of the telephone, *did* hear the voice of an assistant, Charles Tainter, 213 metres away, linked only by a beam of light, and he *did* wave his hat. We have both their words for it.

During his British sojourn (which made him realise how American he'd become) Bell helped establish the G.P.O. telephone network. But he was glad to return to America in November of 1878. His first daughter had been born in England, and two sons and a daughter would follow her, but of these, only daughters Elsie and Marian survived infancy — which is why the Bell dynasty died out.

Alec's only regret on leaving Britain had been the grandeur of the Scottish highlands, and so it was a stroke of the utmost good fortune which made his father Melville take the whole family for a sentimental journey to the Newfoundland whose climate had saved his own life half a century before.

Alec and Mabel fell in love with rugged Cape Breton Island, and in 1886 bought fifty acres and a rudimentary house which they started re-building as a summer home. For the next 36 years, he, Mabel and the girls, with husbands when these arrived, would spend each summer there, in *Beinn Breagh*, or Beautiful Mountain.

(Gaelic was one of the few accomplishments denied Alexander Graham Bell. He had to look this one up.)

We have no space to describe this extraordinary man's experiments with aeroplanes, the phonograph, telephony, hydrofoils, an iron lung — and even the development of a new breed of sheep on Cape Breton, with more nipples, to feed more lambs. I like to think of him, huge, handsome and rather overweight, sitting at a grand piano, either in the Cape Breton house or in Boston, playing and perhaps singing, to a rapt audience.

He certainly wouldn't like to be remembered as simply the inventor of the telephone. 'I am a teacher of the deaf', he maintained to the end (and, right to the end, he was somehow fitting this in with his other work). Much could be written about his efforts with deaf, dumb and blind Helen Keller, and a suitable epitaph for the man might well be Miss Keller's dedication of her book, 'The Story of My Life':

'To Alexander Graham Bell, who has taught the deaf to speak and enabled the listening ear to hear speech from the Atlantic to the Rockies, I dedicate this story of my life.'

His death came during one summer visit to *Beinn Breagh*. He'd been mysteriously weakening for some time and in the early morning of 2 August 1922 his pulse just stopped. A moment before, as he lay on the bed, Mabel had spoken his name and his eyes opened. 'Don't leave me,' she said, and he smiled. Then he gave the familiar deaf-and-dumb finger clasp for 'No'.

He was buried there, on Canadian soil, at his beloved *Beinn Breagh*. But, as he'd insisted, there was a small inscription on the tombstone, with the seven words, 'Died a citizen of the United States'.

His beloved Mabel survived him by only five months, and was buried at his side. They had only daughters, so the family name has not survived — except in the Alexander Graham Bell Association For The Deaf, and the enormous Bell Telephone System with its hundreds of millions of subscribers.

And in the hearts and minds of uncountable deaf people, who are able, thanks to this man, to lead almost normal lives.

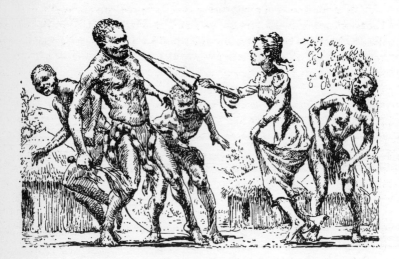

Mary Slessor

It is the face of a humorous, intelligent girl of the nineteen-eighties. The hair is cut short like a man's, and the smiling eyes set well apart in that oval, handsome face, with the high cheek-bones, have an almost oriental look about them.

Only the leg-of-mutton sleeves which one notices after one has stared into the face itself, only these set Mary Slessor firmly in the nineteenth century.

When she was forty-three — which is some time after this particular photo was taken — a young man of twenty-five died of a broken heart because she refused to marry him. Perhaps men don't die of broken hearts, but Charles Morrison pined away, was invalided out of Africa, grew steadily worse and died while trying to recover his health in North Carolina.

She converted blood-streaked savages twice her size, by rushing at them with her umbrella, beating them over the head. She dealt with the sex life of cannibals. She went everywhere barefoot.

A man at one of her lectures, when she was on furlough in Scotland, would upset her so much that she would ask that he hide himself behind a lady: in Africa, she was surrounded, unmoved, by naked men; watched sex orgies of a sort to make even our own permissive age gasp in horror. Calmly, she went on to explain to ageing savages, after her umbrella had stopped them beating their young wives, just why it was natural that those wives should feel an urge to fly into the jungle with younger men. She explained, too, after hundreds of years in which twins were killed at birth as being the result of union with the devil, that only a man of the utmost virility could produce two at a time; she brought pride, lasting joy, to parents — and life to twins.

She died in 1915, and her name in West Africa means more even than David Livingstone's, more than those of others who gave lives to the Dark Continent. Livingstone was almost a saint (though in some ways he was less than human, as the death of his wife bears out): little Mary Slessor was as human as they come, and within the narrow geographical limits in which she worked (no explorer, this girl) she was as fine a missionary as ever lived.

She came from Aberdeen — and if readers may be noting that we seem to include a fair number of Aberdonians, may I assert that I had no idea, till I began to study the little missionary I admired, that she came from that Granite City. And perhaps Aberdeen has little cause to be proud of its connection with Mary Slessor, for she lived in a slum and was reared by a drunk. Slessor was a cobbler and the sad little sums he earned in the shoe factory were squandered each Saturday, so that when he awoke on Sunday to the sound of church bells and an inner clanging of the skull, it was to discover that a handful of coppers stood between his family and starvation by the end of the week. Mrs Slessor went out to work to keep that starvation at bay; one by one the children started dying.

Mary was the only one to survive into old age, and few of the six even reached adulthood. She was born in 1848. Her mother was a God-fearing woman who pinned hopes on her eldest, Robert:

Robert would be a missionary. But he died at the age of sixteen, at the same time that his father was sacked from the shoe factory. They decided to start a new life, move to Dundee.

The mixture in Dundee was much as before. Mary, now ten, was a half-timer in a factory (as were others, at other times, in these pages), doing one day's work among the jute, and another at school. A little later she was doing twelve hours a day, every day, in the jute mill — and, exactly like the man she most admired, was propping a book against the loom to study. Just like David Livingstone.

The second son, John, the one who would be missionary after Robert, died two years after him.

Suddenly, Mary realized she was the one; she, Mary Slessor, must become the family's missionary. And in an instant she had chosen not only her vocation, but the scene of her endeavour. It would be Calabar, on the west coast of Africa.

There is, in the way they decided exactly where they would work, and insisted on it, and in what they did when they got there, a striking resemblance between Mary Slessor and Gladys Aylward, the 'small woman' missionary in China.

Why had Mary chosen this unhealthy coastal region?

Because of the odd, fascinating way the Calabar mission had sprung up. It was an area rich in slaves; the land on both sides of the Calabar estuary in Nigeria teemed with potential slaves and many men had made fortunes in the trade. (In fairness to the white man, it must be pointed out that the slave trade throve long before he got there, with African tribes busily selling themselves and their neighbours into slavery with other African tribes and with the Moslems of the north.) It was an occupational risk to a white man that if his slaver were wrecked on the coast he would be butchered by the natives.

And so, when the slave ship on which Dr Ferguson was ship's surgeon perished in a tornado, and the wreck was flung against the shore, a terrified crew hid themselves in the jungle.

Africans came in their hundreds to loot what was left. After a few days, with the hulk picked dry, they vanished, but by this time the white men were dying like flies of disease, starvation, crocodiles.

Then, round a bend in the river, came a war canoe. The wrath of

Africa was better than starvation and the survivors waved and shouted.

The war canoe picked them up, took them to a native king. And he made them welcome. The white men were nursed back to health, taken to the nearest port. When the next English ship came in, they were taken back to England.

Dr Ferguson was profoundly moved by all this — as well he might be. He determined to set up a mission, in token of his gratitude. And eventually, after many difficulties (the ungrateful blacks didn't *want* a mission), Calabar was set up, in 1843.

The natives, though reasonably friendly with these white inter-lopers, persisted in two deplorable practices. They massacred wives and slaves when a great man died; and, as we have seen, they slaughtered newly-born twins. These were just two of the wrongs Mary Slessor was determined to put right.

But for several more years there was no opportunity. Her father died, her mother was ailing, the survivors of the family, apart from herself, were too young to work: she had to keep the lot.

She was twenty-six when David Livingstone died — and now, with two other sisters just old enough to work, she could go out, take his place. She would send home money from Africa, she would need none herself. Her mother agreed and Mary went to the Foreign Missions Board.

The Board wrinkled its brows over her insistence on going to Calabar and nowhere else, but they gave their permission.

She sailed on the *Ethiopia* of the African Steamship Line. A humdrum voyage was livened by a squall as they rounded the western bulge of Africa, but all of it, squall included, was fascinating to a young girl just out of Scotland. They came to the estuary of the Calabar river, entered it. There were canoes everywhere, so it seemed the *Ethiopia* must run them down, feed shouting black men to the crocodiles, but they dodged the ship and went on shouting.

The villages of Old Town and Duke Town came in sight. They dropped anchor and the Mission Boat from Duke Town came out to them, a white thing with an awning, propelled by four native rowers in neat shirts and trousers, with a prim pair of missionaries, one of each sex, in the stern.

They came aboard, introduced themselves as Daddy Anderson and his wife, Mammy.

Ten minutes later, Mary Slessor was on the soil of Africa, in the Duke Town Mission grounds. There were twelve white people and a large number of doubtful African converts helping in the work. She was shown her tiny white-washed room. There were prayers straight away, in the Efik language, and an unrehearsed — and therefore terrifying — lecture by Mary ('Right, my dear, you tell them all about yourself, *now* —') which was translated, sentence by sentence, from broad Scots into Efik.

And almost immediately young Miss Slessor shocked everyone. She laughed, she sang, she ran races with the natives — and, horror of horrors, she climbed trees! She was a scarlet woman: it was made clear that unless she buckled down and made herself an example — of the proper sort — to the heathen, she would be bundled off home.

There was less tree-climbing after this, but Mary continued to go for long walks, often alone, finding out what she could about the savages — and, much as she learnt to love and understand them, they were this and worse — and their customs. Every rich man had slaves, she saw, but the slaves for the most part were happy and well-treated.

She noted with disapproval the absurd European clothes of the Mission ladies, their hats, their veils, their long, wide skirts. She resolved, just as soon as she dared, to go hatless, shoeless, petticoatless.

One day early on, when she was out walking, miles from the Mission compound, there was an outbreak of *Egbo*, the hateful cult which came to the surface from time to time. When it did, people were murdered, tortured, mutilated.

A gong sounded — and the village through which she was passing seemed to empty itself in an instant.

Into the emptiness burst a naked woman. She was screaming, a high-pitched, terrifying sound; and seconds later a huge man, painted from head to foot, rushed at her with a ten-foot whip. She screamed, ran faster, stumbled, fell.

Other men, in various stages of undress, ran in from the jungle, all with whips. One seized the woman by a leg, started dragging her towards a hut.

This was too much for Mary Slessor. Clutching her umbrella, she tore into the centre of the village. A painted, naked man stared at her in amazement, then slashed with his whip. He missed, she got in under his guard, dealt him a murderous blow with the point of the umbrella. He groaned and she brought it down with all her strength on the top of his woolly, mud-streaked head. He staggered off, and the others, after watching open-mouthed, went too. The whipped woman crept away.

The Mission, when it learnt, was horrified.

By 1880, after one home leave, she was back in charge of Old Town, at her own request. Here she would be away from other missionaries, able to get on with the job as she saw it. She lived alone in Old Town, which, despite its name, was a small and stinking village on the river bank, a few miles away from Duke Town and the Mission.

On the surface, Old Town's inhabitants were law-abiding, but everyone knew atrocities still took place in the blackness of the jungle. These Mary would deal with, but in the meantime, away from the primness of Mission life, she cropped her hair like a boy's, discarded shoes and underwear. And, of course, stays. The first Mission visitor to come her way was aghast at finding her in the shapeless mother Hubbard prescribed for the modesty of African ladies.

She set about building her community. There would be a church here, a school there — and until she had trained her helpers she would officiate in both. And, of course, in the hospital.

Shortly after her arrival in Old Town, she attended a birth. She came barefoot, carrying towels and antiseptics, to find everyone in the hut dead drunk, except for the pregnant girl who lay spread-eagled on the filthy mud floor, held tight by four women, while a witch doctor postured above her.

As Mary took in the situation, another woman appeared from nowhere, straddled the girl and jumped with all her weight on the distended belly.

Amid screams, a child was born.

Then to more screams and a deadly silence, another.

Half the people in the hut tore out into the night. Mary, shaking her head with annoyance, knelt down to look after the girl and her twins. After she had cut the cords and made the mother as comfortable as possible, she quickly wrapped the tiny black babies in a cloth and ran back to her own compound.

Her family of adopted children had begun. The real mother was never seen again.

From now on, every sort of horror descended on her. She watched a man, tied to a stake in shallow water, being eaten by a crocodile. He was only a slave, sacrificed to improve the fishing, and she had been too late to save him. She was too late to save a number of other men, women and children from similar hideous fates. But she did succeed in rescuing the two young wives of a chief. They had been caught in adultery with slave boys and would have been indescribably mutilated, savaged with knives and boiling palm oil, before being put to death. Mary Slessor, eyes flashing with rage, stopped the ceremony before it began.

'*Stop that!*' she screamed. It stopped as if a thunderbolt had struck the village.

Then, recovering her composure and her breath, she explained that this sort of behaviour was absolutely forbidden and that *she* would not permit it. As for the erring girls, she would deal with them herself.

As for the pot-bellied old lecher who kept wives locked up because his own attractions were insufficient to keep them at home, he was beneath contempt. Was he not ashamed of himself? Was he a man, able to hold his women like a man? Or was he not?

There was shocked silence, then laughter. The meeting broke up in confusion.

She had found that here, in her own community, she was able to live on the proverbial smell of an oil rag; with tidy Europeans in Duke Town, it had been expensive, paying one's share of unnecessarily lavish catering, keeping oneself respectable. Now, in Old Town, she was able to send her salary home.

But in 1886 her mother and the last surviving sister, Janie, died. Mary Slessor was thirty-eight and alone. And now there was no reason for not going up-country, to the dangerous, forbidden areas, where no white person had been. She was a missionary, and although exploring held few attractions for her, she knew her job was to look after the bodies and souls (in that order) of the African people. Those who most needed her help were a hundred miles inland, murdering each other.

After much argument, the Mission said she might move to the Okoyong district. Mark you, they pointed out, it was entirely at Miss Slessor's request. On no account was she to involve the mission in expense.

And so she moved north, by canoe. An interesting sidelight on the character of Mary Slessor is that she was throughout her life terrified of canoes, snakes, wild beasts. But it never hindered her in anything which she knew was her duty. She got to the land of the Okoyongs and they were unable to believe this lone white woman would dare to move in among them. She did, and they accepted her with reluctance.

Then, when they saw she would teach their women to cook properly, to care for their children and to sew, they made her welcome.

There were dreadful occasions when, despite the promises she had wrung from them, they slaughtered their slaves and their wives, broke the arms and legs of children and threw them screaming into their mother's graves. She saved many, many lives — but there were many for whom she was too late.

But in the end she was successful — and successful where probably no other missionary would have been. Living with them, completely as a native — yet keeping herself scrupulously clean as an example to them — she was able to understand their thinking, get inside it. Before she left Africa the practices she abhorred had been done away with.

There had been undeclared war between these inland, bush people and the coastal Calabars, for hundreds of years, since the advent of slavery, when the Calabars had started raiding the bush for slaves. Now Mary Slessor began what had always been thought impossible, began to open up the inland region to peaceful trade.

She travelled a great deal, visiting hidden villages, helping and teaching their inhabitants, and the years crept by. For the most part, other missionaries left her alone to get on with her work, but there was one young man who began to pay regular visits from the Duke Town Mission.

She was forty-three — and Charles Morrison was twenty-five. He asked her to marry him.

She considered it. Of course, he would have to come and settle among the Okoyongs, there was no question of her going back to the Duke Town Mission — or anywhere else. He agreed: he was eager to come. And it would be convenient, too, for the continuity of the work; they could take their furloughs separately, thus ensuring that one or other was always there, ready to deal with the sudden, life-and-death emergencies which arose so regularly.

The Mission authorities, who regarded Okoyong as a dubious hinterland, came to the decision that Charles Morrison could not be spared from his work at Duke Town.

Perhaps they made a mistake. For Morrison, from that moment, went steadily downhill. His health, his work, grew worse: he was sent home. He got better: the doctors advised against his returning to Africa. He resigned, went to North Carolina, died.

But, husband or no husband, Mary Slessor had need of an assistant. The work, the bouts of fever and dysentery, had aged her. She asked for one or more female helpers, and her appeal gives an idea of the sort of woman she herself was. She wanted women, 'not afraid of work or of filth of any kind, moral or material. Women who can nurse a baby or teach a child to wash and comb as well as to read and write; women who can tactfully smooth over a roughness and, for Christ's sake, bear a snub. If they can play Beethoven and paint and draw and speak French and German, so much the better, but we can want all these latter accomplishments if they have only a loving heart, willing hands and common sense. They will not need fine English, for there is none to admire it —'

She dealt, almost single-handed, with a smallpox epidemic which wiped out nearly half her community — and her problem was a thousandfold worse than that of a doctor in less superstitious lands, for she had to avert the orgy of human sacrifice which was waiting to be unleashed to appease the sickness devils.

She was shipped home, sick and weary. A year later she was back, and now, having civilized Okoyong, she went on into still less tractable lands, to cannibal country. She went, amazed the cannibals, won them over.

But this indomitable little creature could not go on for ever. She became crippled by arthritis, suffered constant fever. At last, in 1915, she died.

What had she done? What had she achieved, apart from the saving of lives in a land where life is cheap?

Many things. Above all, she completely altered the status of women in her part of Africa — and the movement is still spreading. She civilized a part of the world unique for its barbaric cruelty, a savagery with which Livingstone hardly came in contact. She left behind a nucleus of hospitals and schools which are a credit to all Africa.

She died, as she would have wished, among the people to whom she had given her life She was buried, while hundreds wailed and tore their clothes, at the Duke Town cemetery.

In Nigeria — and elsewhere — the little, short-haired barefoot woman with the flashing eyes, the eyes that sometimes smouldered, often laughed, will never be forgotten.

What would Stanley have made of her, this faintly comic little figure in a shapeless mother hubbard, brandishing her rapier of an umbrella? 'Mary Slessor, I presume?'

But even without Stanley to make a journalistic legend of her, Mary Slessor stands as monument to generations of selfless missionaries who lived and died for Africa.

Robert Louis Stevenson

They say he should never have married; that the fine, tender, blossom of Stevenson's thought was crushed by the cares of matrimony and a materialistic woman. Fanny Stevenson — what a name for a start! — was both a divorcee and an American, never a popular combination in the British press. In order, they said, to keep herself in the comfort to which she had been accustomed, she forced him to write at ever-increasing speed, even getting her son, his stepson, to collaborate with him from time to time, just to speed up the process and get things to the publisher. She killed him, and he died of overwork at the age of forty-four.

This sort of tale, simply because it *is* malicious, dies hard. But, of course, it is utter nonsense and about as far from the truth as it is possible to imagine. The legend of R.L.S. abounds with nonsense: let us deal with this bit first; and let the others, as we look at the man himself, speak for themselves.

After he met Mrs. Fanny Osbourne in France, and after he subsequently married her, he wrote almost everything for which we remember him. *Jekyll and Hyde*, *Catriona*, *Kidnapped*, *Treasure Island*, *The Master of Ballantrae*, for a start.

Before that he had written a handful of essays, *The New Arabian Nights*, and *Travels with a Donkey*.

With his stepson, Lloyd Osbourne, he wrote, among other things, *The Wrong Box*, ultimately made into a hilarious film; also *The Wrecker* and *The Ebb Tide*. With Fanny, he wrote *Dynamiters*, a sequel to his early *New Arabian Nights*. For to Stevenson, the business of writing was an exciting, technical challenge. He was a stylist: the game, like a superior crossword puzzle, was one he eagerly shared with others.

The pictures extant show him for the most part with hair which would have done justice to a nineteen-sixties' pop group. Though the face amongst all that hair is too sensitive, too intelligent for us to envisage behind microphone or guitar, the effect is misleading. Why these photos are almost the only ones no man can tell: we know there were others taken during the last four years in Samoa, photos of a wiry, short-haired man chopping down trees, galloping on horseback, doing a thumping great job of gardening in the early morning before settling down to a full day's writing, and apparently thriving on it.

As for his youth — and we have few pictures of that either — it must have been quite unlike the long-haired invalid of the pictures, with the wan and pallid smile. (Though that youth may well have contributed to the serious illness of middle-age; for the young R.L.S. was a rip and a rake, and worse. His father, dour lighthouse designer, who had so wanted this literary-minded son to take after him and dot the coast of Britain with beacons, was appalled.)

R.L.S. was born on 13 November, 1850, in Edinburgh. Both father and grandfather were designers of lighthouses. From birth the boy was sickly, prey to every wandering germ, so that he spent much of his childhood in bed. It was this that reluctantly decided his father not to try and make him a lighthouse designer: the open-air work would kill him.

And yet, when the family moved from Edinburgh to the Pentland Hills, the boy spent most of his time on long walks with his father, and loving it.

He went on to Edinburgh University to study Law and, at least for the time being, forgot about the writing which, since childhood sickbed, had been such a hobby. His health had improved: there seemed no reason why he should not make a success of his studies.

But he behaved disgracefully. It would have been disgraceful anywhere, to say nothing of within that stern, Calvinist environment. Edinburgh is not a town one thinks of in terms of the brothel industry, but there were sufficient in Stevenson's time, and he found them all.

Somehow he managed to get his Law degree. Fortunately for the legal profession, and certainly for that of letters, he never practised it. Almost immediately he fell seriously ill, which is hardly to be wondered at. And it was while he convalesced with cousins in England that he met two people who were to have a considerable effect on his life: Mrs Sitwell and Sidney Colvin. They urged him most strongly to become a professional writer, go where his talents and interests led him. Colvin was instrumental in getting his first work, *Roads*, published in a magazine.

For this first professional contribution, Stevenson signed himself as others did by initials. R.L.S. was to become a signature for the rest of his life. In some quarters this was seized upon as affectation: who did this man think he was? Was the world expected to bow down before three little letters, know whose they were?

Stevenson survived this sort of thing and more. But in the meantime, his health still in need of repair, he was packed off to the south of France. He went on writing, and at his return was able to offer essays to the *Cornhill Magazine*, essays which were eagerly accepted and which laid the foundations of his career.

In 1877, aged twenty-seven, he went with his cousin Bob Stevenson on a long ramble over northern France. Much of this was by canoe along inland waterways and formed the basis of his first book. It was published the following year under the title, *An Inland Voyage*.

And it was during this summer that he met an attractive woman, considerably his senior. She was from Indiana and she was staying at an inn in the Forest of Fontainebleau with her two children. He fell instantly in love with Fanny Osbourne and with the children, Isobel and Lloyd.

He also fell on his feet. For his love was returned, and he was able, while the spirits of Calvin and of Knox spun furiously in their graves, to move in with her. He spent the next two summers with her, his winters in Edinburgh. He was happy and he wrote a great deal. His reputation grew.

He was distraught when Fanny decided to go back to her husband in California, but tried to make up for the loneliness of the next summer by going on a long, lonely trip in France with a donkey — an expedition which produced the attractive *Travels With a Donkey* in 1879.

And in that year he made his wild dash to California. He had learnt that Fanny Osbourne was seeking a divorce from her husband: if this were so, he was determined to marry her himself. His friends and his parents were appalled: everything about the proposed expedition, from its length and his health, to the moral turpitude of both California and Fanny, made it outrageous.

Not only that. The career in Law, which his parents and R.L.S. almost believed he might take up, would be finished if he cut adrift now.

He cut adrift. As he had little money, he travelled to New York by steerage on the ship, which made him as ill as he had ever been. He followed this up by immediately crossing the entire continent in an emigrant train of unexampled squalor, and arriving in the West nearly dead. In fact, he was given up as lost by physicians in Monterey and in San Francisco, but managed to thwart both.

By the time he got to Fanny, having kept himself alive by writing what anyone would buy, he was a doomed man. Not, however, as doomed as the California doctor assured him. All medical opinion pointed to the certainty that this gaunt Scottish scribbler would be dead within the year, aged thirty. He married Fanny and survived another fourteen, to the age of forty-four. By this time he had done more great work than most writers do in far longer lives.

From now on, though he never made complete recovery, he had

the loving care, the inspiration — and the money — of a devoted woman to keep him alive and writing. He had feared that after the furious separation from his father and mother the year before, the mad dash to America, they would never speak to him again, but a reconciliation came about and he returned to Scotland with his wife and young Lloyd. His parents fell in love with them both.

Although the intention was not to return to America, they soon found that Stevenson's lungs were unable to stand the damp and cold of Scotland for more than a few months at a time. He and Fanny began to spend summers in Scotland with his parents and winters in Switzerland. It was in order to amuse a rather bored young stepson during a miserably wet summer afternoon in the Highlands that he began work on an adventure story. He finished it after many interruptions, many months later, in Switzerland.

He decided then to call it *Treasure Island.*

Young Lloyd enjoyed the book which had been written for him, but not everyone else felt the same way. Its publication by Cassells in 1885 brought fame and fortune to the author — yet it is not so generally known that its first publication, as a serial in the magazine, *Young Folks*, was a flop. None of that publication's young readers enjoyed it.

Like many other writers, Robert Louis Stevenson was able to keep two or more irons in the fire at once, and while he amused himself in finishing this tale of adventure he embarked on a labour of love, *The Memoir of Fleeming Jenkin*. Jenkin had been the Professor at Edinburgh University who had stood by him — as Stevenson put it, 'in the coiled perplexities of youth' — and known that somehow, inside the debauched body, was a beating heart and a genius.

In that year, 1882, he and Fanny moved to the south of France, and though his health became critical again he wrote most of the *A Child's Garden of Verses*. As a sick child he had had a nurse, and it was to her that he now dedicated the work: 'From the sick child now well and old' — in a mood of brave exaggeration.

Then, still unwell (and he would never be old), he rushed home with Fanny to settle in a house at Bournemouth. They had learnt that his father's health was failing; were resolved to stay near the old man for however long his illness lasted: the south coast at Bournemouth was as close to Scotland as R.L.S. dared live, if he himself were to survive.

Three years went by, in which he was an invalid, almost always in bed, and his father died. Nevertheless he managed to write *Kidnapped* and *The Strange Case of Dr Jekyll and Mr Hyde*, two huge and instantaneous successes, which arrived in the nick of time, when his fortunes were at their lowest ebb. The latter book appeared in America and gave such joy (as well it might; it had been pirated) that he was persuaded to go over again, with his mother, Fanny and Lloyd, to face his admirers. The strain was too great, however, and he found himself seriously ill again, trying to stage a recovery in the Adirondacks.

To this pleasant resort we owe *The Master of Ballantrae*. As we have seen, he loved sharing the game of writing with others, and it was here that he and Lloyd plotted the hilarious *Wrong Box*.

A sudden stroke of good luck — which probably earned him a few more years of life. His American publishers asked him to do a travel book on the South Seas, gave him a handsome advance. With this he was able to charter a yacht and sail — still with mother, Fanny and Lloyd — from San Francisco into the wide, uncharted spaces of the South Pacific.

Scotland's climate has driven many good Scotsmen from her bosom. To that fact we owe the invention — in America — of the telephone by Alexander Graham Bell, and the development in England by another fervid Scot, John Logie Baird, of television. And Robert Louis Stevenson is one of the best examples of this trend. From the moment he embarked on the chartered *Casco*, his health changed dramatically for the better. Within a week his bewildered, delighted family found it hard to realize that this energetic, wiry man of thirty-seven, bounding about the decks, rushing inland at each port of call to strike up improbable and lasting friendships with dusky rulers, was the invalid who had embarked at San Francisco.

From this week on, though in fact mortal illness was still with him, the long-haired invalid was a thing of the past. It was too hot for long hair, and it came off: the pallid dreamer's face grew brown, and jollier with each new friendship.

So enthusiastic was he that, having paid off the yacht and sent it home, having sent his mother back to Scotland, he stayed in Honolulu with Fanny and Lloyd for a further six months. They began taking passage here and there in other vessels, eagerly investigating the unknown lands to the south-west.

And it was on the island of Opolu, one of the Samoan group, north-east of Fiji, that they fell in love with the place and bought an estate. It was beautiful and balanced halfway up the side of a blue and shimmering mountain. He and Fanny would divide each summer between England and the Continent — with winters on the island.

Fate stamped on this plan within a month. They were on their way home for the summer of 1890 when another serious bout of illness flung him into a hospital bed in Sydney. This time there was a major haemorrhage of the lungs and the doctors were adamant: not only could Mr Stevenson not continue his journey to northern lands; he could never go there again, if he wished to survive a few more years.

Life for Stevenson had always been a series of jerks, blows and surprises, good and bad. This was just one more. He accepted the verdict calmly, sent Lloyd on to collect the family furniture. Then he went back to his island and started to re-build the house on his new estate, the estate which henceforth would be his home. He named it *Vailima*.

The next four and a half years — his last years — would be as fruitful as any in his life. His mother followed Lloyd and the furniture to the South Seas, and a little later Stevenson and Fanny were joined by Fanny's daughter Isobel, who was now grown-up and married. She brought husband and small son. Surrounded by a devoted family, his health began to recover and he started another series of writings, which included *Catriona* and *The Ebb Tide*.

For these last years he was a Samoan laird. He was happy, healthier than he had ever been, and with nothing but a few money worries to disturb him. Many of these worries were unjustified, but Samoa is a long way from the nearest publisher, and he worried often about his sales, his royalties, and all the things that authors do concern themselves with. (Though most authors are able to put themselves out of their misery in rather less than three or four months.)

The Samoans worshipped their laird and he became deeply involved in their troubles, to the exclusion of his own. His Samoan involvement embraced everything from local politics to full-scale war. He managed in the intervals of this life to begin and continue a long correspondence with J. M. Barrie, a correspondence that ended only on his own death, and to Barrie's deep grief. He had discovered an article the younger man had done about him in *An Edinburgh Eleven*, and wrote, tongue-in-cheek, chiding him about it. Barrie was thrilled; wrote back by return.

Pilgrims came, literary pilgrims from all over the world, much as they had gone to Abbotsford. The trip was far longer for most of them, but still they came, devoted ones and twos, to *Vailima*.

He had cheated death for years — but it caught up at last. On 3 December, 1894, he was shaving when he suddenly turned round from the mirror and said, 'Do I look strange?'

Before an answer could be given he fell down. Cerebral haemorrhage.

He died immediately after, was buried on the mountain he loved, Mount Vaea.

As we said at the beginning, there is a remarkable absence of Stevenson portraits near the end of his life. Perhaps nobody in Samoa had a camera. But when the familiar photo, with the long hair and the pallid face, was shown to a small Samoan boy who had known the original, he squealed with rage:

'I will not have that — it is the face of a pig, a pig! That is not the shadow of our chief!'

A statue was erected in his memory at Edinburgh. Not at first, for there were many good burghers still deeply shocked by the poet's behaviour at University, by his action at running away with — or was it *after*? — a divorced woman. Barrie and others fought for the statue, and at long last it went up.

But the real Stevenson was thousands of miles away. We Scots may claim him as our own, but he was happiest in Samoa. Perhaps

he had never been happy anywhere before, happy and well. Above
his grave on Mount Vaea are the words he wrote as his own epitaph:

> *'Under the wide and starry sky*
> *Dig the grave and let me die:*
> *Glad did I live and gladly die,*
> *And I laid me down with a will.*

> *'This be the verse you grave for me:*
> *Here he lies where he long'd to be;*
> *Home is the sailor, home from the sea,*
> *And the hunter home from the hill.'*

Keir Hardie

Saints are pretty thin on the ground in politics. Indeed, sanctity and politics are about as incompatible bedfellows as we could invent.

Perhaps bearded, horny-handed, trouble-making, old Keir Hardie is about as close as we have come, in this century, to having one in the House of Commons.

I would probably have voted against him, were I voting in any of the several constituencies he represented during his career; but I would probably have respected him more than the man who got my vote.

He was born on 15 August, 1856, in a one-roomed house — not the two-roomed luxury of Ramsay MacDonald, on another page — near Holytown in Lanarkshire. He was the eldest of nine children, with a father who was a ship's carpenter and a mother who worked on a farm. It was from this mother, Mary Keir, that he derived not only his name but all the education he acquired before reaching manhood. Apart from a few, isolated, months he never went to school. His mother taught him to read, taught him the Christian virtues: his father was a fervent, dedicated agnostic, yet he imparted a habit of intellectual honesty which stayed with the boy all his life, and would enrage others throughout it.

He worked at a variety of jobs, earning pennies, until he went down the mine, aged ten. Here he was happy, for the miners were kind, good friends, and the fact that for months on end he seldom saw the sun did not distress him. He was underground by six every morning, up again at five; and working a part of every Sunday as well. His first work below ground was driving a pit-pony, Donald, for whom he developed a real attachment, with whom he shared his bottle of cold tea.

Later, as muscles and frame expanded, he was made coalhewer, hacking the stuff from the seam. But by now there were other thoughts in his mind: he was twenty, he had seen so many drunken men abuse their wives, squander their wages in a night's debauch, that he began a campaign for temperance, a drive against drunkenness.

He also gave much thought to Christianity. He had experienced the hypocrisy of those who went to church on Sunday and had family prayers at home, yet didn't care whether their servants or employees starved. He'd had his own vivid personal experience of this, working for a bible-thumping baker. But he was still a devout Christian and he began to preach on street corners, urging, not just temperance, but the word of God.

The word of God — yes: its advocates on earth — no. 'They have never,' he wrote of the clergy, 'have never originated any great movement. Whether it be the abolition of slavery, the abolition of the drink traffic, the abolition of child labour; no matter what the question, the pulpit has always kept aloof until some mere worldling has educated the public and made the new cause safe, profitable and respectable.'

A stinging indictment — and written in anger. 'There have been splendid exceptions, but these only serve to bring the facts as here stated into more general prominence. That the masses will in time be quickened into a healthy state of activity, I have no doubt; but when that time comes, it will be the work of Socialists, not of the clergy, which will have brought it about.'

No wonder many hated him. But let us go underground again. Ironically, it was here that the mine-worker came nearest to being at peace with his world. There was good-humoured comradeship, even laughter, and the miseries of poverty in an overcrowded one-room cottage could be temporarily forgotten in the all-embracing dark. But Keir Hardie knew that something must be done, some day, about the miners' life, and it came to him, down the mine, that he might be the man to do it. By his own exertions he was now, at the age of twenty, far better educated than any man in any mine in Lanarkshire — and his workmates knew this, began to listen to him when he spoke, to adopt him, almost unconsciously, as their leader. If a meeting were held to discuss some real or fancied grievance, Hardie was pushed forward to take the chair.

Soon his name, to the mine-owner, meant Labour Agitator. He was sacked. But in fact the most that Keir Hardie wanted — though it may have seemed like heaven then — was a living wage for miners, better conditions of safety under the ground, and some sort of better accommodation above it. Miners in Lanarkshire almost all lived in one-room houses, with their entire families, and Hardie was right in seeing this as an affront to civilization. On the other hand, the mine-owners were not too far from the truth when they protested that most miners were 'quite content with their lot'. Ruefully, Hardie would bear this out in an anecdote he constantly re-told. It was a true story of the cheerful miner's wife who was asked by a visitor where she did her washing, her cooking, and the rest of it, in that one room. Where, for that matter, did she and the family sleep?

The miner's wife patiently pointed out the various corners of the room where these functions took place. And, in any case, it wasn't bad; there were only two wee bairns so far.

'But what will you do when there are more?'

'Och, that?' She smiled. 'We'll just tak' in a lodger tae help pay the rent.' And she meant it.

The mine-owners maintained that without agitation from

'professisonal trouble-makers' like Keir Hardie, life in a mining community would be peaceful, prosperous and happy. And before we scoff at this, for it is obviously quite wide of the mark, let us look at the words of another miner of the period, from the same mines. Harry Lauder — whose story is on another page — wrote, years later: 'I was a member of the Lanarkshire Union of Miners, a strong supporter of men like Keir Hardie. But politics were not mixed up in industrial affairs as they are today. Besides, there seemed to be a far greater measure of freedom for a man to work as hard as he liked and as long as he liked for the benefit of his own payroll and the increased comfort of himself and his family which the fat payroll represented. With few exceptions, every man in the pit in those days was a hard, conscientious worker. He worked hard, and he played hard. I would not go the length of saying that we were all contented with our lowly lot, but we seemed to believe in the old Scriptural injunction that only by the sweat of our brows could we eat bread. And by God, we sweated right enough!'

A point of view, and perhaps conditioned by time and prosperity; a fatter 'payroll' than any miner could dream of. But worth noting.

Keir Hardie was glad to leave the mine: there was more time now to plan on the miners' behalf. He started a small shop and at the same time became local correspondent of a Glasgow newspaper. He still talked at street corners, but now, rather than press the virtues of temperance, he harangued the miners, pointed out their disabilities, told them what to fight for, how to fight. He advocated no violence — but he called for unity, and with it strength. The response was slow. There were too many Harry Lauders down the mine.

He married, moved into Ayrshire, to the town of Cumnock, and there became editor of the local paper, the *Cumnock News*. At the age of thirty he realized one of his dreams: an Ayrshire Miners' Union came into being, with himself as secretary. By this time he had become disenchanted with the Liberal Party, of which he had believed himself a supporter, for the Liberals, even those who styled themselves Radical and were more Liberal than the rest, were remarkably like Tories. Perhaps this was not surprising in the days before a Labour Party, even before a Labour movement, because no M.P., whichever label he affixed to himself, was paid a parliamentary salary, and therefore, with a few, specially subsidized, exceptions, only a rich man could be a Member of Parliament.

Hardie stopped writing for Liberal newspapers. He could see his goal: he would get the representatives of real working men into Parliament. He might be their representative himself.

At this time Scottish miners were taking home twelve shillings a week. Depression had set in over all of industry, and there was hardship everywhere, not only among miners.

He left the *Cumnock News*, founded his own paper, *The Miner*, in 1887. It became the mouthpiece for his views, Keir Hardie's forceful point of view, with an ever-growing readership — and a name that changed, within twelve months, to *The Labour Leader*. He was convinced, now, that he must get into Parliament. There were a few other men of similar background to himself, within those august walls, but they were supported by Party or other funds which virtually deprived them of freedom of action. As he now wrote in *The Miner*, this type of M.P. was not a success, 'because he is afraid to offend the proprieties by being considered extreme. He thinks more of his own reputation in the eyes of the House than of the interests of his suffering brethren in mill and mine. He desires to be reckoned a gentleman fit to take his place as a member of the first club in the world.'

He stood at a Lanarkshire by-election in 1888 and received a tenth of the total votes. He would have to wait for another opportunity.

That opportunity came in 1892 — and to many social historians it marked, eight years early, the start of a twentieth century. He was adopted for Independent Labour by the London borough of West Ham, and got in. It was not a Labour Party that he represented: merely the idea, the novel idea, of working men, men who Laboured, being in Parliament and quite Independent of any other party.

So his was a party of one. His arrival at Westminster to take up its duties has gone into history. The other Members of Parliament arrived, most of them in carriages, most wearing silk hats, whether they styled themselves Liberal or Conservative. They nodded politely to each other: after all, it made no difference whether a chap was Liberal or Conservative, he was still a member of the Best Club in the World.

And suddenly into this scene, like a Go-Kart sputtering on to the course at Ascot, came Keir Hardie.

The noise of his arrival was at first so deafening, so upsetting, that no one took notice of its appearance. The loudest trumpet in Christendom was playing, at the top of its owner's lungs, a tremendous, home-made fanfare. Then, as the vehicle came to a halt, the trumpeting stopped.

The stunned audience noticed now that it was a large, two-horse wagon — the horsed equivalent of our Utility trucks, and less than fashionable outside the Palace of Westminster. As it stopped at the gate, a bearded man, stocky, near middle-age, and dressed in tweed suit with cloth cap, hopped nimbly down and went in. The wagon with its load of cheering workers, its trumpeter, drove off.

So entered history's first 'Labour' Member of Parliament — a number of years before that Party came into existence. Many, but by no means all, M.P.s were affronted by this 'blatant self-advertisement' of a man with a trumpet and wearing, of all things, a *cap*. Anyone, even this chap, could have borrowed or hired the right rig.

In fact, had the soft hat he ordered arrived in time, the cap which caused such a stir would never have been seen.

He was a man without a Party — but by 1893 he had formed one: the Independent Labour Party of all men, inside or outside Parliament, who believed in the idea of labour being independently represented, being kept clear of the two major parties. He was the first Chairman of this ILP: one of the first members to attend meetings was George Bernard Shaw.

He lost his seat in the election of 1895, but a year later was returned for Merthyr in Wales — and this community went right on electing him throughout the rest of his life. By 1900 it had become obvious that though people in Parliament listened and sometimes took action when he spoke or asked questions there must be more than one solitary Labour man in Parliament. The

Trades Union Council called a meeting to devise means of getting more of them in, and the Labour Representation Committee which was born at that meeting was the real ancestor of what we know as the Labour Party.

The Committee did its work well, and in 1906 no fewer than twenty-nine Labour members — one of them, of course, Keir Hardie — entered Parliament. The Labour Representation Committee proudly changed its name to the Parliamentary Labour Party. It has never looked back — and all the good or evil, depending on your political views, which that Party has brought mankind, dates from that day in 1906.

But what of Keir Hardie, its founder?

He went on doing exactly what he thought was right. History may prove some of this to have been very wrong, but he never budged an inch from his principles. He was the virtually unique, entirely honest politician. To this extent he treated political opponents as personal enemies; could never see — or never saw — that one could be friendly with a man whose principles one deplored. He agitated for working-class rights, votes for women, Home Rule for Ireland. He went on publishing *The Labour Leader*, which remained the vehicle for his most biting comments. With it he fought the slippery Horatio Bottomley, just acquitted, for the third time, of fraud. When Bottomley wrote angrily that he would not have his honesty brought in question, *The Labour Leader* wrote: 'It must be a source of the greatest satisfaction to a man that he has the verdicts of three juries to certify that he is not dishonest.'

At this point Bottomley conceded the argument by default.

The South African War came, and Hardie lost sympathy in the country by his vigorous objection to it. He had forgotten that Britain is a country ruled by Fashion, and that while a fashionably large minority will declare for Pacifism (or Nuclear Disarmament, or the Abolition of the Royal Family, or what you will) under favourable circumstances, a change of circumstance — like war — which reduces that minority by a large percentage, will result, overnight, in its baffling disappearance. Hardie advocated Pacifism — and many agreed — but when the time came to implement it he found himself quite alone, with Press, Public, snarling. He refused to alter his point of view.

Unlike Ramsay MacDonald, he remained through life a Pacifist; there was no question, ever, of supporting a war, just because, like Mount Everest, it was there. He fought war, and the idea of war, with every means at his disposal, and he was — not without reason — branded a traitor. To Keir Hardie the most beautiful thing in years had been the scene he witnessed during the Russo-Japanese war, when fraternal delegates from Russia and Japan to the new Socialist International had embraced in public. The fact that, even as they hugged, a few thousand on each side were being slaughtered, and both huggers knew and cheerfully accepted the situation, was far too Machiavellian for Keir Hardie to understand. The Socialist International made no difference, the war went on. And as the years went by, and he aged prematurely through overwork, Keir Hardie grew bitter.

He believed, unlike MacDonald, that Marxism would prevent war. It was simple: the workers of the world would go on strike, the war would end.

The 1914 war came, and nobody, at least at first, went on strike.

But this was incredible. Surely with the Weapon to Stop All Wars right at hand it would be used?

It was not — and the shock, the disillusionment, killed Keir Hardie. He protested feebly, angrily, about 'the roar and song of a war-maddened people', and these very people, his ardent supporters of a week before, booed at him, screamed at him. He was a traitor, an enemy of his country.

On 26 September, 1915, he died.

He had done great things — and perhaps some harm. He had founded a Labour movement, a long-overdue Labour Party. Had he lived another nine years he would have seen what he so long dreamed of, a Labour Prime Minister of Great Britain.

And, because he was a saint and a simple one, it was easy for others less saintly to follow cynically in his footsteps, to organize, to destroy. It has been said that Keir Hardie unwittingly lit the fuse which was to destroy Scotland's ship-building industry. For a start.

Only time will tell if he did.

Sir James Barrie, Bart.

The Scots work hard, play hard (when there's time), strive more than most, perhaps, for success. Every one of them in this book achieved it, though success may have been short-lived or sown with the seeds of disaster.

But, surprisingly, the successful authors among them were, almost all of them, brilliant amateurs. In other words, they regarded themselves as essentially something quite different, and writing as their hobby. That they beat the full-time professionals at it is beside the point: Buchan was a lawyer — and as for Byron, just being Byron was a career in itself.

But one was the most dedicated of professionals. He made up his mind at an age when most of us are struggling to spell out one-syllable words (and hating it), that he would be a writer of words. And absolutely full-time, to the exclusion of all else.

So he was. Not just a struggler in a garret, but the proverbial household word, who at one time was pulling in almost fifty thousand pounds a year, entirely from his literary exertions — and in a period of time when that sum was worth far, far more than it is now.

And this was without assistance from the film industry. There wasn't a film industry.

His reputation, as well as the real value of his earnings, has depreciated in the years since his death. Earnest Scotsmen — and there is nothing so earnest as an earnest Scotsman — have derided the sentimental Kailyard School of which he may be regarded a founder (and which we touch on, as indeed Buchan did, with venom. in the Tweedsmuir article). But literary fashions change and there seems no reason at all why J. M. Barrie should not one day be rehabilitated, as Dickens has been.

To millions of now-grown-up children he is still the father of Peter Pan. For real, nineteen-eighties children his position is less assured; the whole idea of a magic boy standing at the front of a stage and getting the audience to agree it believes in fairies is far removed from the world of the telly. Not that Barrie didn't people his world with all sorts of terrifying creatures, fully as frightening as the wickedest bad-man in a Western. It was this that captured the children; their parents wept over Peter.

But one doesn't go on making fifty thousand pounds a year just on the strength of one good play. James Barrie's output was very large indeed, and much of it is well worth our attention today.

If Barrie had been only a lovable little man, devoted to children, a man with an uncanny knack of writing for them, there would be little point in including him here. But he was more and less than this; an exceedingly complex creature.

He was born, more than a century ago, in the small town of Kirriemuir, Angus, some twenty miles in from the east coast of Scotland, and north of the Firth of Tay. And Kirriemuir, of course, is the Thrums of his novels. He was born in an absurdly small cottage, and was the ninth child to be born there, though two, by the time of his arrival, were already dead, and the eldest away at Aberdeen University. The date was 9 May, 1860.

David Barrie was a weaver who worked at home, on a piecework basis, and how he found space to work, to say nothing of earning sufficient to keep his large family, is still a mystery. But he did, and with his wife was able to instil a love of learning and a zeal for education into all of them, so that Alexander, the eldest, not only won his bursary to Aberdeen University, but went on afterward to a distinguished career in education.

Like some others in this book, the Barries had long seceded from the Established Church of Scotland. They were members of the Original Seceders or Auld Lichts (lights of purity, no less), and young James's uncle had risen from the same artisan stock to be Doctor of Divinity.

There was tragedy, too, in those early years. To get some idea of what life was like in The Tenements, Kirriemuir, we can do no better than look through James Barrie's book about his mother, *Margaret Ogilvy*. It is a sentimentalized account, but even in this cynical age it isn't hard to shed a tear over it.

But back to the boy. With everyone in the family helping, including free board with the eldest brother, Alec, who was conveniently teaching there, James went on to Glasgow Academy. The fees at this excellent school were less than £5 a year, but still a great sacrifice for a father with other children for whom he planned the same thing. James did well at the Academy, but he had to move from it when his brother changed jobs.

By this time their father had become a clerk and been able to buy a larger house, *Strath View*, still in Kirriemuir. Alec had got a better job in Dumfries and the arrangement was renewed so that Jamie now went to Dumfries Academy and boarded with him there. Probably these school years really *were* the best years of his life, the only time when he was entirely happy: he liked writing stories; he liked being a boy. Dumfries was the last time he was able to indulge both simultaneously.

Peter Pan was still thirty years off. In the meantime, Jamie contributed to a school magazine and acted strenuously in a drama group. 'I came out strongly as a young lady, with my hair tied to my hat.' He even wrote several plays for it, in one of which 'I played all my favourite characters in fiction, artfully rolled into one'.

There were girls, too, in Dumfries Academy, and as time went by Jamie found them attractive. (For some odd reason they were not allowed into the drama group, and boys still had to tie their hair to their hats.) As for the girls from other schools in the town, whom he met at tea-parties, some of them 'looked so soft that you wanted all at once to take care of them'.

He did, too. And this attractive quality about him was almost to destroy him, many years later.

It has nothing to do with that prognosis — but James Barrie was now sixteen years old and five feet one inch in height. He went on from sixteen, but his height remained constant. Perhaps this was the closest he could get to staying a child.

To Edinburgh University, aged eighteen. He worked hard (unlike Stevenson who had been there a year or two earlier) and emerged as James M. Barrie, M.A. — still determined to enter one of the few professions where this distinction would be of no use.

He began to bombard the press with articles, suggestions for articles, suggestions for books. Just as one wonders how Buchan the story-teller managed to produce his tome on *Taxation*, one finds it hard to reconcile the author of *Peter Pan* — or *Dear Brutus*, or *The Admirable Crichton* — with his suggested *Early Satyrical Poetry of Great Britain with some Account of the Manner in which it illustrates History*. Nor, for that matter, *A Queen Dowager in Love*. Neither was ever written.

It was his sister, Jane, who turned the tide of rejection slips. She was the only member of the family who believed in the wisdom of setting out to become a writer pure and simple. To the rest he was only 'wasting an M.A.'. And it was Jane who saw the tiny advertisement in the *Scotsman* for a leader writer on the *Nottingham Journal*.

He got the job: he was twenty-three.

The *Nottingham Journal* was one of three local morning dailies at the time, and, like the Three Little Nigger Boys, soon there'd be two. It was owned by a pair of brothers who knew nothing of running a newspaper, but had private means, and within a few years it had sunk without trace. (Though the name has been revived since.) But for two of those years it was a splendid training ground for young Mr Barrie, who wrote profusely for it, in different styles on different subjects. Sometimes he was anonymous, sometimes *Hippomenes*, sometimes *A Modern Peripatetic*. Always he was readable.

He also fell in love, in a hopeless way, for the first of many times. He wanted to 'look after her', but probably he was more in need of that assistance himself. She vanished.

By 1884 he had had quite a few articles accepted by London journals. After some had been taken by the *St James's Gazette*, he seized time by the forelock and wrote to Frederick Greenwood, the editor. He enclosed an article with the unpromising title of *The Rooks in Dumfries* and suggested that he might move to London: all he would need was a little encouragement.

Stony silence; followed, many days later, with curt advice to stay where he was.

At which point James Barrie bought his single ticket south. On the night of 28 March, 1885, he took the train to London.

His impertinence — there seems no other word, so let us make a fine haggis of our metaphors — his impertinence bore fruit. In a remarkably short time, having calculated he could live on £1 a week, he was making two or three times that amount. In later years a pink haze of sentiment obscured those first months in London, and he wrote that he lived near starvation on penny buns. He pointed out that this young and foolish J. M. Barrie had — instantly on disembarking at St Pancras — bought himself a silk hat, with which to impress editors, though it cleaned him out of money. Other evidence from himself and his friends contradicts all this (in any case, he arrived on a Sunday) and it seems a fact that he made a reasonable living from the day he arrived. He had already given himself a flying start because *The Rooks Begin to Build* appeared on Saturday, 28 March, in the *St James's Gazette*.

Soon he was making a good living out of journalism alone, and finding time to begin the longer work on which his heart was set. He had found with Greenwood and the *St James's Gazette* that anything with a Scotch setting usually sold (and to the end of his days he refused to use the newfangled word Scots). His first long works, blending family and Scotland in a fairly thick gravy of sentiment, were *The Little Minister* and *A Window in Thrums*. Before this he had produced and sold *When a Man's Single* and *Auld Licht Idylls*. Always he worked on a number of projects at the same time — and by no means all of them were sentimental or even respectable. It was years before he published it, but he wrote and re-wrote a mock-serious attack on various personalities of the day, *The Case for Doing Without Some People*, which annoyed them all.

He had met, on the *Nottingham Journal*, a fellow-Scot, Thomas Gilmour, who had preceded him to London and done well for himself straight away by not only remaining a journalist but becoming Lord Rosebery's secretary as well. Gilmour was probably the greatest friend Barrie ever had, though they quarrelled often. He was certainly a good friend, with infinite patience, for Barrie steadfastly refused to open a bank account for himself and for years demanded that Gilmour cash all his cheques, which he sent to him in bundles every few weeks. ('Do not trouble about the odd pennies — ') Eventually Gilmour could stand this no longer (or perhaps it was his wife, for the showdown took place soon after his marriage). Barrie was taken firmly to a branch of Barclay's Bank and made to open his own account.

(But Barrie's lack of interest in money matters was notorious. Once he was embezzled out of £16,000 by a theatre manager and never noticed it until others took legal action on his behalf. There is a sad sequel to that story, for while Barrie was prepared to forget the whole thing, didn't want his money back, the others pressed the case, and the man committed suicide.)

In 1892 — catastrophe. Not, perhaps, for a different sort of man — but what seemed catastrophe, the end of everything, for James Barrie.

His much-beloved younger sister Maggie was engaged to be married to a young clergyman in Caithness. Barrie had gone up to Kirriemuir on holiday with her, and was almost as excited as Maggie about the approaching wedding. They went for long walks together, chatting about the way Maggie would decorate her manse, how often Jamie could come up and visit. He had a bit of a proprietorial interest as he had given the young minister, Jim Winter, a horse to help him get round his far-flung parish.

They got back to the house in Kirriemuir to find a telegram. Jim Winter had been killed instantly, flung from the horse Barrie gave him.

Barrie was appalled; he was entirely responsible for the tragedy; he had presented the horse. Maggie collapsed.

And now for weeks they sat together in this darkened room in Kirriemuir, both of them in an agony of grief, and Barrie 'looking after' his sister. He took her completely under his wing, sat with her day after day, making sure no one came in to interfere with her grief. There would be no question now of his ever marrying: he would give up his life for Maggie.

Six weeks of this at Kirriemuir, guarding his sister, comforting her — and then he decided they must move. He got the loan of a cottage, near Guildford, and took her there.

At this point, mercifully in time to take his mind off his troubles, he got the first, thrilling letter from Samoa. Robert Louis Stevenson, the great R.L.S., had written from all those thousands of miles away, written to comment on a somewhat impertinent essay about himself which Barrie had included in the book he wrote on leaving Edinburgh University, *An Edinburgh Eleven*. Good-humouredly, Stevenson wrote that he had just discovered the work and read it: he had 'a great mind to write a parody and give you all your sauce back again — '

Barrie was as excited as a schoolboy. Grief was forgotten. (Which was as well, for as soon as he stopped reminding her of her sorrow, Maggie made a fine recovery.) He wrote back immediately, and the correspondence between the two, R.L.S. and J.M.B., went on until Stevenson's death. In the course of it, Barrie looked up Stevenson's relatives in Scotland; Stevenson urged him to come and stay in Samoa.

When he was thirty-four, Barrie married an actress, Mary Ansell. It was, on the surface at least, a happy marriage for a number of years. There wasn't a great deal of 'looking after' to do, for Mary had a mind of her own and plenty of resource. They moved to Kensington and she set to work making her house and garden the height of fashion. Already people turned to look at them in the street; and now the house in Kensington was pointed out in awe, for Barrie's first full-length play, *Walker, London,* had appeared and been a success.

The novels of Scottish life poured forth: *Margaret Ogilvy* (about his mother); *Sentimental Tommy; Tommy and Grizel.* His *Little Minister* was dramatized (eventually bringing in no less than £80,000). He was an assured success, and rich.

He turned full-time to writing plays. This is hardly surprising, for, as we have seen, he was fascinated by drama at Dumfries Academy and after; he had fallen in love with many, many actresses; and succeeded in marrying one for himself.

And then, over the Christmas season of 1897, the Barries met the Davieses. No one knew it at the time, but the pattern of all their lives was changing.

Sylvia Davies was beautiful and talented. She was the daughter of George du Maurier, the artist and writer. She was happily married to a struggling barrister husband, and when the two families met, she and Arthur Davies had three small sons, the youngest of whom was called Peter. The Barries had only an enormous Newfoundland dog.

The parents grew ever friendlier, and at the same time the Davies boys became fascinated by the little man, this friend of their parents, and particularly of their mother, whom they met each day with his Newfoundland dog in Kensington Gardens. Sometimes his wife was with him, more often not. He was a tiny little man and lots of fun.

As for the three boys, they were eager youngsters, full of life, and they wore unusual little square-necked blouses which their mother made for them. (Soon these blouses would be seen on the London stage and copied all over the world.) The little man told them exciting stories as they strolled by the Round Pond.

This friendship heightened that of the parents and soon the Barries and the Davieses were in and out of each other's houses, on opposite sides of the park, almost every day. Or to be more accurate, Mr Barrie was in and out of the Davies house, dragged there by the adoring boys.

Arthur Davies seemed to tire of this: he knew that Barrie was far richer than himself, that the boys loved him, that his wife thought him amusing. He, of course, trusted his wife, but it was only too obvious that, once again, James Barrie had fallen under the spell of a beautiful woman. Of course, there was nothing serious, but it was irritating, just the same.

And at this point we leave this promising parallelogram to note that *Peter Pan* was produced in 1904 and was, as everyone knows, a staggering success. The American producer Charles Frohman had been offered two plays by Barrie on his visit to London and accepted both. One had been still untitled, just *A Play*, the other was called *Alice Sit by the Fire*. Frohman liked them both, proposed putting on *Alice* first. But the London theatre he needed was booked for the autumn and he plumped for *A Play*, a thing about fairies and pirates which obviously must be a Christmas production.

The first night was 27 December, 1904. By this time, *A Play* had been named *Peter Pan, or the Boy who Wouldn't Grow Up* — and there can hardly ever have been a more instant success. The first shrieks of delight were heard when Nana the Newfoundland (so like Barrie's) picked up Nicholas Darling's nightclothes: the shrieks, the applause and the laughter kept up until long after the closing curtain.

The critics liked it, too. But there was one dissentient voice among them. A critic, confronted by this stage-full of children, had muttered, 'Oh, for an hour of Herod —'

All that is history. The play went to America, did just as well there. The sort of money that started rolling in made it possible, as we have seen, for a theatre manager to fiddle the books for many thousands of the playwright's money, without his noticing. Apart from this, the years went by happily, prosperously.

And one morning something delightful and odd happened. A statue of Peter Pan was unveiled in Kensington Gardens, very close to where, as half the world now knew, James Barrie and his big Newfoundland dog had strolled with the three Davies boys, one of whom was Peter. What a charming idea, that a lover of Peter Pan should have erected this memorial to the boy who never grew up!

But when it was discovered that the statue had been erected by Barrie himself, eyebrows rose.

He made a great friend now, Robert Falcon Scott, who was as fascinated by the genius of the playwright as Barrie was by the bravery of the explorer. Barrie and his wife introduced Scott to his future wife, a sculptress, and later J.M.B. became godfather to Peter Scott — today's naturalist — the only child of that marriage.

And, still later, a tragic letter from Scott to this dearest friend gave details of the South Pole expedition in which he perished.

But now, back to our parallelogram, our Davieses and Barries. Much had been happening. Arthur Davies, just becoming successful and wealthy as a barrister, died of a terrible cancer of the face, leaving Sylvia and the boys destitute. (And there were now *five* boys, not three.) So Barrie, much as he had done with his sister Maggie, began to 'take care' of the family. He had sat bravely — and lovingly — by the dying man's bedside: now he adopted the survivors.

It was a selfless act, but a foolish one. He cheerfully took on a heavy financial burden, helping educate the boys, keep them all in the manner to which they had been accustomed. He did his best to comfort and cheer the widow (and this is not said with sarcasm or innuendo: he did just that).

But Mrs Barrie fell suddenly in love with a much younger man. Why? Because her foolish, kindly husband had planned and taken a holiday on the Continent: two Barries, six Davieses, plus a young man he had recently met to even up the sexes of the adults. The holiday took place, seemed successful. Everyone returned happy and healthy to England and their respective homes.

Barrie was told the truth a few months later by his gardener; and Mary Barrie, who might have been planning to run away with her lover, was suddenly confronted by a distraught husband. He would forgive adultery, forgive anything, but she must not leave him.

She did and he was forced to grant her a divorce. The shock and the scandal nearly killed him. He moved, a completely broken man, to the Adelphi (built by Robert Adam and his brothers, on another page of this book), and had as his neighbour George Bernard Shaw.

Slowly he recovered from the shock, the disgrace. He went on, of course, subsidizing the Davies family as before, getting one son into Eton, another (recommended by Scott) into the navy, and so on.

Perhaps he and Sylvia considered marriage, but that future now ended with Sylvia's death, as tragic as her husband's.

James Barrie was in charge of five growing boys and minus a wife to help him: he shouldered the burden without complaint. It told on him; the lines on his narrow face grew deeper and deeper as he worried more, worked harder. But that work never faltered, and a stream of successful writing poured from his pen over these years: *What Every Woman Knows, The Twelve Pound Look, Dear Brutus.*

In 1909 he refused the offer of a knighthood — and his public were impressed that here was a simple man who wished to remain plain Mr Barrie to the end of his life. But, rather as with the discovery of the donor of the Peter Pan statue, the public was disappointed in 1913 to find that the higher offer of a baronetcy had been accepted.

The work went on — and with it fame mounted. In 1922 he got the Order of Merit, that proudest of all British honours, with a total membership of only twenty-four. In 1930, to his great joy, he was made Chancellor of his old University.

On the other hand, old friends were dying. This grieved him terribly; each death was a personal tragedy. His own health began to fail, slowly but steadily, until in 1936 there came a triple shock. His biblical play, *The Boy David*, flopped disastrously; his life-long friend, the casher of cheques, Thomas Gilmour, died; and he himself, for the first time in his life, was seriously ill.

There is one touching and attractive episode to brighten the last sad months. He had been one of the great for years, had come in contact with the Royal Family and in particular had struck up a friendship with little Princess Margaret, still a child. He had slipped into the mouth of Elisabeth Bergner, star of his ill-omened *The Boy David*, some felicitous phrase which Margaret had spoken when they met: later he told her of it, gleefully confessed his plagiarism, promised a royalty. Perhaps the idea of Royalties-for-Royalty amused him: at any rate, Princess Margaret's would be a penny a performance.

There were, alas, not many performances. The abdication of Edward VIII more or less coinciding with the first night of *David* was partly responsible for its death. But now the new king, George VI, did something imaginative and kind, exactly tailored to the idiosyncrasies of the dying playwright. He professed to be angry that no royalty had been paid, and a tongue-in-cheek missive came from the Palace. If Sir James Barrie did not immediately honour his agreement, he would be hearing from His Majesty's Solicitors. It was quite possible that His Head Would Be Chopped Off.

This — as George VI knew — was exactly what was needed to kindle the spark of life. Barrie got better immediately, arranged for a proper legal settlement to be drawn up by his solicitor, and for the — very small — royalty to be handed over by himself in newly minted pennies. He would, of course, require a Royal Receipt.

The game went on, the preparation of the Document took him out of himself, and for a while it seemed he might recover. Then, when his secretary sensed he might not, the Document was sent to be signed at Buckingham Palace: the bag of pennies would follow, just as soon as the Debtor was well enough to deliver them.

He never was. The Document came back, signed and with many kind messages. But Barrie was never well enough to complete the transaction, and he was determined no one else should. He died, after a long illness, on 19 June, 1937.

To the world Westminster Abbey seemed the obvious resting place, but Barrie had been definite about this. His body was taken north to be buried beside the rest of his family at Kirriemuir.

It had been a long life and — perhaps — a happy one. James Barrie left behind many, many things for which we have cause to be grateful. He died before that second great war which would change the life he had known, sweep it away and substitute something quite different.

Which he would never have liked or understood.

Ramsay MacDonald

He was the most unpopular man in his country: hated, despised, by all political parties and most people. He was a turncoat, a Socialist who had 'yielded to the temptations of the aristocratic embrace', a bolshevik, enemy agent, tool in the pay of foreign governments. The lot.

His almost unbelievable rise from rags to riches, from the humblest of childhoods, of which he very naturally made good use in politics, is quite true. Rather more remarkable, if we look at it, than other climbs up the ladder of life in this book.

Time has thrown the man, and what he did, into some sort of perspective. Not only is his a famous life: it is in many ways a great one.

Unfortunately for the biographer, almost all Ramsay MacDonald's achievements were political, and politics, even if the

performer is alternately a 'bolshevik' or 'yielding to the temptations of the aristocratic embrace', can be deadly dull.

We will try to see the man as he was. With Ramsay MacDonald, I
think the man is more important than the politician.

Hard up against the Moray Firth, not too far from Inverness,
where as the inhabitants know the only perfect English in the world
is spoken, there lies the small town of Lossiemouth. Those of us
who live in, or visit, the hills to the south of Huntly tend to view
Lossie askance. For one can be terrified out of one's wits by the
sudden explosive arrival of a supersonic jet from behind a grouse
butt or belting up the roadway like an airborne cow. Yes, the Vale
of Huntly is in the Low Flying Area of the Royal Air Force Station,
Lossiemouth, and men have been known to collapse in ditches, the
word 'Lossie!' on foam-specked lips.

But a hundred years ago, Lossiemouth, and the whole of that
chunk of northern Scotland, was at peace.

In one household, however, as summer slithered into autumn,
the heather blossom faded and the first days of October passed,
there was trouble. Isabella Ramsay, middle-aged, work-weary,
deserted these years past by a shiftless husband, had brought up
four young children in this two-roomed cottage. Now, all too soon,
another mouth would come to be fed. Isabella's youngest daughter
Anne had worked at a farm outside Elgin and been seduced. She was
now with child by the head ploughman and in a few days' time that
child would be born.

They regulate most things well in Scotland, and, of course, the
father — though Anne refused to marry him — would give his name
to the child. The kirk might frown upon fornication, but it
happened, and often. There was no question of young Anne being
flung out, metaphorically, into the snow. She would deliver her
child with all the help and care her family could provide. And they
would help her look after it.

The boy was born on 12 October. The year was 1866.

Later in life he was to remark — and some would think it
boastful, many would think it untrue — that extreme poverty of
the kind he had been born into tended to 'breed the aristocratic
virtues'. Certainly the normal Scottish urge to learn, be educated,

succeed, flowered to an unusual degree with young James Ramsay MacDonald. His mother was able to provide the eightpence a month needed for him to attend the village school at Drainie, and here he swallowed learning at a prodigious rate. Anything, as long as he could understand it: arithmetic, history, all the usual subjects, plus the unusual choice for a small boy in a village school: literature in Latin and Greek.

Partly this may have been an hereditary urge, for his grandmother had books, a surprising number of them, in her cottage. And her daughter, James Ramsey's mother, had been acknowledged the most intelligent of her four intelligent children.

There was another man of letters in the neighbourhood: the watchmaker had his library, which Ramsay devoured in slices, like cake. It goes without saying that he was the star pupil of the Drainie School. In fact, when the time came to leave, the dominie urged him to stay on as pupil teacher. There would be a salary of seven and a half pounds a year.

During the two years that Ramsay MacDonald held down that job he read and absorbed more than most men do in a lifetime.

Perhaps it was just the sort of books the dominie had: MacDonald seems to have read every social history in print and to have decided, then and there, that he must be a social worker. The term is a portmanteau one, of course, and every Member of the House of Commons (and of the Lords) is as much a social worker as the youth club leader. For Ramsay MacDonald it would be social work of one sort or another for the rest of his life.

At the end of two years' teaching and reading he headed for England. He had read an advertisement for the 'right sort of man' to organize a young people's club in Bristol.

Here, quite by chance, for this was just about the only city in England with such a thing, he found a Socialist organization. There was no such thing as a Labour Party in those days and he eagerly joined this Social Democratic Federation in Bristol. At the same time he developed his latent taste for geology: in the intervals of running his youth club and attending meetings of the S.D.F. he took up the serious study of this science.

This included the purchase of books about it. Within a few

months Ramsay MacDonald had returned to Lossiemouth, poorer than he had ever been — and armed with a totally useless knowledge of geology.

Another suitable-seeming job was advertised, in London: he made haste to get there. Unfortunately, this one had gone by the time he got there, and unlike James Barrie, who was able to start earning a living immediately, MacDonald very nearly, and literally, starved. No one was interested in an uncouth lad from the north. However well-read he might be, no one could understand a word he said, for a start. In order to keep himself alive he got his family to send down oatmeal (for which he paid, when he had the money), and with hot water he made porridge.

Sometimes the only water available was cold: then it was sawdust in the mouth, but he ate it.

At last he got a job. A little later he got a better one. Neither had any bearing on social work — or even science, which had now become an obsession. Once again he spent his available money, after sending some to Mother, on science books. Once again he had to creep back to Scotland, half-starved, health and finances apparently ruined.

But now his fortune changes. He recovers his health and a little later is back in London, doing a job he really enjoys, being Private Secretary to a Parliamentary candidate. He is with him for three years, coming in contact with all sorts of people, all sorts of political thinking. At the end of the period he is able to keep himself in some comfort by writing for Liberal newspapers. There are no Labour papers.

Suddenly, Ramsay MacDonald discovered a new and civilized form of Socialism. He became a Fabian — and his attitude to social reform changed accordingly.

The Fabian Society — named after the Roman general, Fabius, The Delayer, and therefore pledged to fulfil its aims gradually — had been founded two years before, in 1884, for 'the advancement of Socialism by democratic means'. It was against all forms of 'revolutionary heroics' — and young MacDonald found this a novel and pleasing point of view. Not only this: the Fabians, like Mac-Donald, were dead against the various irrelevant cults, from free-love to theosophy, which had slipped in under the umbrella of Socialism. They — and he — wanted justice, fair play, for the poor and less fortunate: anything else was a distraction.

On the other hand, though Fabians might demand a rational approach to Socialism, though the man-in-the-street was beginning to think he might want Socialism, there was no hope of Fabian egg-heads — like Bernard Shaw — converting the proletariat. However worthy their motives, no one would listen to them.

Had it not been for the birth in 1893 of the Independent Labour Party (not independent of the Labour Party, which didn't yet exist, but independent of the other two big parties with which, perforce, the labouring man had been allied) Socialism would probably never have come to Britain: it was all too remote, too silly.

And so we have MacDonald as an avowed, even accredited, Labour supporter, growing steadily in the estimation of others like himself, so that in 1895 he is even allowed to contest a Parliamentary seat as I.L.P. candidate at the general election. Catastrophic defeat — which was all he expected — but marvellous experience.

Another landmark: he now married a girl from a different, very different, social background. She was a great-niece of Lord Kelvin, and her name was Margaret Gladstone. No relative of the politician Gladstone; but her father, as well as being a scientist, was a social worker. As these were Ramsay's chief interests, the two men must have been drawn to each other.

Margaret had become attracted to Socialism — no doubt this is the reason she married him — and she became a devoted, loyal wife: MacDonald would need that, in the years ahead: though, alas, they would share very few of them together.

His wife also had an income of her own: from now on he need not scribble away for newspapers whose policy he disliked. From now on the pair of them would do what they could for mankind — through the Labour movement.

A house in Lincoln's Inn Fields, and quite a new social horizon. Sherry parties of Fabians, tea-parties of trade unionists, the constant planning of Utopia By Democratic Means. He was able now to travel, and over the next few years he wrote thoughtful books on what he had seen and thought. Two of these were *The Awakening of India*, and *What I Saw in South Africa*. The former is one of the best books ever written about India.

Nearer at home, he dealt knowledgeably, provocatively, with *Socialism and Society*.

And in 1906 — Member of Parliament for Leicester. The Labour Party was born this year. Whatever MacDonald might have styled himself before, he was now the Labour Party Member for his constituency. Most of the twenty-nine Labour successes in this election came as a result of a pact with the Liberal Party — and this fact must be borne in mind when screams of 'turncoat!' and 'renegade!' are heard in a few years' time. He was soon risking a great deal: in 1911 he became leader of the Labour Party and three years later had enraged the whole country by opposing Britain's entry into the First World War.

By this time personal tragedy had struck. His youngest son died and, a little later, his wife. He wrote a tribute to her and this was later published, as *Margaret Ethel MacDonald* — a moving and revealing piece of writing.

But now, in 1914, because of his supposed attitude to the war (in fact, now it had been declared he wanted it fought hard, and finished), he was the most hated man in Britain: a pro-German and a pacifist (he was neither). At the end of that year he joined an ambulance unit and got as far as Belgium before being brought home.

Unfortunately for Britain, and in particular for MacDonald, the Germans were able to make good propaganda of what he had once said. This distortion of his views made certain that he would be hated by everyone in Britain. He was.

A next opportunity for getting himself hated came in 1917. In March of that year the first Russian revolution took place, under the moderate, Kerensky. MacDonald loudly applauded this. (And had the aid which he so shockingly wanted to offer Kerensky been permitted, that mild and beneficent regime might have been able to stay in power, not be obliterated by the Bolsheviks.)

At the General Election in 1918 he was defeated at Leicester by a staggering margin.

After having worked four years behind the scenes — but sometimes very much on stage, as Labour Party representative at conferences abroad — he got back into Parliament in 1922. He was now Member for Aberavon, in Wales; and he was immediately elected chairman of the Parliamentary Labour Party. Two years later he made history — with Liberal support again, let us not forget that important fact — made history by forming the first Labour Government.

Probably he should never have allowed himself to become Prime Minister, for he now made the great mistake of trying to couple the duties with those of Foreign Secretary. Without doubt he was better at the latter. Domestic affairs, and therefore the future of himself and his Party, got steadily out of hand.

1926 — the General Strike. MacDonald, having failed to avert it, fell in with the aims of the strikers, though hotly repudiating both violence and Communism.

Three years later, as a result of a marathon speaking campaign in which he travelled to every part of the country and held meetings, Labour was returned, with an absolute majority for the first time. He himself was returned for Seaham, in County Durham.

Still his main interest lay in foreign affairs. He was a great believer in personal contact between Heads of State, and in the same year he made the first visit of a British Prime Minister to a President of the United States. (I was eight at the time, living in America, and I clearly remember the excitement I thought I felt at having our Prime Minister over: the pictures of lantern-jawed Mac and pie-faced Hoover standing affably together.) MacDonald was no longer allotting himself the role of Foreign Secretary, only devoting most of his attention to that job. Understandably his hold on the Party and the electorate began to loosen again.

And now, in 1931, still more disgrace. Recession — depression — had come and there was so much disagreement within the Parliamentary Labour Party over steps to combat it that MacDonald had to rush to the King and say his colleagues just couldn't agree: they were thus not an effective government. He tendered the Labour Government's resignation.

At his Sovereign's request, MacDonald now formed an all-party coalition government — and while a large slice of his own Parliamentary Party were in hot disagreement over its policy, he yet chose to remain Prime Minister, supervising his hybrid. Lord Passfield angrily accused him of having 'succumbed to the aristocratic embrace' and MacDonald was firmly deposed as head of his Party. But, of course, he was still Prime Minister.

There seems little doubt now that he had one chain of thought in his head: he must stay in office to solve the vexed constitutional crisis; and he must steam-roller through the urgent legislation needed to 'end the depression'. There was no intention in his mind that these strange and kicking bedfellows, the Libs, the Labs and the Conservatives, should stay more than a week or two between the sheets.

Circumstances demanded that they did. And still, while all sides cursed him, he stayed Prime Minister.

Yet in October, when his coalition government appealed to the electorate for a 'doctor's mandate' to do what it thought best for an ailing Britain, and risked itself at a General Election, it was returned by a very handsome majority. And MacDonald himself, rejected by his own Labour Party, was yet returned by Seaham, which had been as solid a Labour seat as any in Britain.

This new Government (still, of course, a coalition) was MacDonald's fourth administration, and although many still complained vociferously that he was a turncoat, should be shot, and the rest of it, the fact remained that he was the chosen head of an administration overwhelmingly returned by the electorate (it had all but fifty-nine of the seats in the House of Commons). MacDonald seems to have handled all members of it with tact and skill, aware, as many Labour people were not, that politics is the art of the possible: that if there were not this hybrid government in charge the country would be in total anarchy.

The threat of Hitler soon appeared on the horizon, growing bigger every month. The British Government set itself to trying to appease the lunatic house-painter — and at the same time getting its own defences in order. MacDonald is often dismissed as an 'appeaser' (and who wasn't, in Britain between 1935 and 1938?), but the important White Paper on National Defence which gave the green light to rearmament was very obviously his own brainchild. It also bore, and still bears, his initials.

But now he was tired, ill, disillusioned. On 7 June, 1935, he resigned the Premiership, handed over to Stanley Baldwin. In November of that year there was another General Election and this time his popularity had waned yet again. He was heavily defeated at Seaham. He had been fully aware that he would be, and in fact regarded his political life as over, but he had courageously agreed to stand to ensure the survival of the coalition government he had originally formed and of the small national Labour group. (He might no longer be P.M. — but he must not leave altogether and imply the ship was sinking.)

Two months later he was returned at a by-election for the Scottish Universities seat, but his career was over. A sick man, he was not involved in the various alarms and excursions of 1936 and 1937 — like the king's abdication — and at the end of 1937 he embarked on a sea voyage to South America in an attempt to recover his health.

He failed. On 9 November, 1937, Ramsay MacDonald died at sea. The body was brought home, and he was buried beside his wife, near Lossiemouth.

Full circle. It is hard to do justice to this outstanding Scotsman, simply because he was so involved all his life with politics — and politics is not the red blood of life. He was, above all, a brave man. (He was dragged back, as we said, from his unauthorized service with British ambulances in 1914, but in fact he got back again a fortnight later as an 'official visitor'. His coolness under fire much alarmed those who were responsible for conducting him, had to stay with him.) His last years as coalition Prime Minister can hardly have been enjoyable, but he stuck it out, to the accompaniment of such abuse as few P.M.s have endured before or since.

He was also a remarkable ambassador. Perhaps he set a bad example, for though he did this superbly (often to the detriment of his political job at home) he led the way for the hordes of little prime ministers, presidents, kings and the like who now scurry from capital to capital doing 'diplomacy', for which few are fitted and fewer trained.

He wrote delightfully, and his two travel collections, *Wanderings and Excursions* and *At Home or Abroad*, are a joy to read. There is little doubt that he might have made a career for himself in diplomacy, literature, or science. Possibly even on the stage, for he had the distinction (within an admittedly poor field) of having been Britain's best-looking prime minister of the twentieth century.

One thing seems certain: he was too good to be a politician.

Sir Harry Lauder

It is axiomatic that Scotsmen do best for themselves when they leave Scotland — if only to cross the border into England. But there are several examples in these pages of those who went much farther afield than England and made great names for themselves. One of these is wee Harry Lauder from Portobello.

In all history there was never a Scotsman who looked or sounded like him — but to the world he was Scotland incarnate.

Certainly he was for me. Fate had decreed that I be brought up, as a child, some three thousand miles away from the Aberdeenshire I regarded as my home. I was happy in New York, but very conscious of being a Scot, eager to clutch at anything which would bring it back to me, take me, if only for a moment, to the land I loved, the land of my fathers.

Which, of course, was a load of codswallop. At the time of which

I write — I was ten — I had no recollection of Scotland at all. But these things are of the mind and of the blood, and during those early 'thirties, in New York (and in Auckland, Sydney, Vancouver and Capetown), there must have been plenty of Scotsmen who knew as little of their native land, and were prepared to weep as hard over it, as I.

There still are.

I listened to Harry Lauder on our big Stromberg-Carlson, with its loudspeaker yards away at the end of a flex, crouching on its little table and echoing round the room. He sang from WJZ — or maybe WOR or WABC — and the tears oozed down my face like steam down a haggis. This was music, real music, and the stuff Dr Walter Damrosch talked about in his Music Appreciation programmes, Mozart and all that stuff, couldn't hold a candle to it. We Scots were a musical race.

What was more, *I* — because I was Scotch — I *understood* what he sang. Thousands wouldn't, over here in the USA, but I was Scotch, and I did.

But, of course, everyone else did, too, from Broken Hill to Boston, Pietermaritzburg to Pike's Peak. There might have been difficulty in the remoter parts of Scotland.

And so the world was fooled — and loved it. This was a real, unspoiled Scotchman, dressed in his native tartan, singing his native songs in his own, artless way. Why, he even couldn't stop laughing at the funny bits; he broke down so helplessly that you felt sorry for him, you loved him. Somewhere along the line the King must have felt that way too, given him a knighthood, for the little wee man was a Sir.

It was one of the most professional, most rehearsed, acts in the world. Every chuckle, every syllable of patter, every catch in the throat, had been rehearsed a thousand times — and it was perfect.

He was born on 4 August, 1870, at Portobello, Edinburgh, the son of a potter who made the stone marmalade jars and gingerbeer bottles which have almost disappeared today. Soon the Lauders moved to Musselburgh to be nearer the pottery, and here, aged five, Harry began his schooling. Unlike others in these pages he took little interest in studies, only in the active world outside the classroom. By the time his father had been offered a better job in the north of England, Harry had picked fruit, been a golf caddie, a feeder of pigs. All this ceased and the family packed to go south with father.

And within weeks John Lauder was dead, of pneumonia. The grief-stricken family, with twelve-year-old Harry as breadwinner, was back in Scotland, in Arbroath, where Mrs Lauder had relatives.

Harry, when he got over the loss of his father, enjoyed being a half-timer in a flax mill — doing one day in the mill and the next at school. He was a towie who collected the tow or thread, after it had passed through the machinery, and got it into a bag. For this work he was paid a little over two shillings a week; not enough, even in those days, to support a mother and six brothers and sisters, but with mother herself going out to mind families, or do other people's washing, they got by.

It was while the family lived in Arbroath that he started to sing. His mother had insisted he join the teetotal organization, The Band of Hope, and he cheerfully agreed because of the music: every meeting ended in song. Now and then boys and girls might be asked to sing or recite something they knew. Harry, suddenly faced with the demand, promptly forgot all the hymns he knew and blurted out a maudlin ditty called 'I'm a Gentleman Still'.

Barefoot, ragged, he was applauded to the echo.

From that moment he seizes every opportunity to perform. At first it is only in competitions (though in the very first one he collects a 'real Abyssinian gold watch' which works for a week and which he cherishes for the rest of his life), but eventually he begins to be paid a few shillings for his services.

There were two years in Arbroath. School was ended now, and life divided itself between the flax mill and whatever village concert might present itself. Opportunities, platforms, were few. Then an uncle urged the family to join him on the west coast, in the mining district of Hamilton. There was plenty of work to be had there, and wages down the mine were better than those above ground. The Lauders moved.

And it was here, down the mine, that Harry Lauder came to the conclusion, quoted in the Keir Hardie article, that mining wasn't a bad job at all. As it happened, both Lauder and Hardie started off in the same jobs: first, as a trapper, opening and shutting a trapdoor to control ventilation; then, as driver of a pit pony. For his work with the pony Lauder got a pound a week.

He got married — to Nance, the pretty daughter of a pit manager. By this time he was supplementing his income regularly with four shillings here, six shillings there, as singer and comic. He had carefully mastered a dozen jokes, rehearsed the telling of them with even more care than the singing of the songs that came between; and financially he was not a bad catch at all. The wedding was the standard Black Country festival of the period and rather gayer than the nuptials of today, for all non-family guests had to buy tickets. For the sum of rather less than ten shillings, a couple could — and obviously *did* — dance, eat and drink till buttons burst, and dawn broke. The happy couple — in this case, Mr and Mrs Harry Lauder — stole away at three in the morning and were never missed. A few hours later they were catching the first train to Glasgow and their one-day honeymoon.

Local concerts abounded in the west, and in most of these Harry Lauder put in an appearance; in most of them — for there was always an element of competition — he won a money prize. Sometimes the prizes were medals, clocks, or vases — even moustache-cups — and these, too, he eagerly competed for. The future was getting clearer: it was all good experience, the chance to learn new songs, new jokes, practise one's patter. Soon Harry Lauder would be a Professional Entertainer.

His biggest engagement of those early days was at the old Scotia Music Hall in Glasgow. Once again there was competition, for if old Mrs Baylis or her patrons didn't like the turn, off you came, usually encouraged by a long crooked stick which emerged from the wings and grabbed you round the neck. One furious artist — this was the start of the Boer War — screamed at the audience, 'I hope the bloody Boers win!' But Harry, trembling with fright in the largest auditorium he had ever seen, was allowed to get through two songs, and asked to come back later. Success at last.

A brief sally into the risky business of being a full-time professional. He took the risk, left the mine, and worked a few months with concert parties. Then the summer season ended, there was suddenly no work, and he crept back to Hamilton. Ashamed, cursing himself for taking a risk with his family's future, he resolved to be a miner for the rest of his life.

The decision didn't last long. Out of the blue came an offer which just could not be refused — a month's tour of the Moss & Thornton Music Halls in the north of England, finishing up with two weeks in Glasgow. It was the last chance, and he took it.

This time there was no doubt at all about it, he was a huge success. He had been practising for hours each evening — as he did for most of his life — and for the English tour he made the wise decision of singing his songs in 'English with a Scotch accent'. To a Sassenach this may seem a contradiction in terms; surely 'Scotch', unless we mean the Gaelic, *is* 'English with a Scotch accent'? But, of course, it is not, and the songs which Lauder had been singing, many of which he made up himself, were stuffed full of words which were meaningless south of the border, indeed meaningless after he had travelled a few miles within Scotland, though he carefully switched some of them around as he travelled from county to county.

From now on — even in Scotland — Scots words were out. The accent itself had to be made clear to the Tynesider, the Londoner, to be clear to men and women in whichever part of the world Harry Lauder might travel. Already he was thinking big.

Later, Harry Lauder described for the benefit of Sassenachs the linguistic complications of travel in Scotland. Like all southern Scots, he points out that the Aberdeenshire way of speech is all but incomprehensible south of that county — a fact which, though from constant reiteration I now believe it, I find strange. To me the language spoken north of the Dee is picturesque and crystal clear, whereas after an aggregate of many months spent in and around Glasgow I can still find myself occasionally unhorsed by the speech of the south-west. But Lauder tells a story of the Aberdonian visiting London for the first time and being fascinated by the lights of Piccadilly Circus. One of the characteristics of broad Aberdeenshire is the substitution of 'f' for both 'v' and 'w', and the question our northern visitor addresses to a newsboy is 'Fit's a'them reed and fite and blue lichties bobbinootaninowerheresee?' The question is repeated several times, with both parties getting more exasperated, until the newsboy shouts, 'Get aht, yer bloody Portugee!' and the interview is at an end.

The red and white and blue lights, bobbing in and out, have fascinated other visitors, too. One of them was Harry Lauder, who bought his third-class single (like half the people in this book) to London. It was March, 1900, and he had gone to considerable trouble to select a wardrobe which would evince both prosperity and talent. He wore, travelling south, a pair of tartan trousers above yellow spats and brown boots. Above this he sported a frock coat and coloured waistcoat. He duly arrived, and such is the sangfroid of England that few people stared. Memories have clouded over, and the various people who recalled meeting him on that eventful day disagree with the wee man and each other as to what he wore, or where he went in it, but one fact is certain. He met Tom Tinsley, manager of Gatti's Music Hall, and was signed up for a turn — just a song or two — that very night.

He was in the dressing-room an hour and a half before he was due on stage. Carefully he did and re-did his make-up, adjusted his highland dress, nervously fingered his stick. When the moment came, he dashed on stage, thumping the floor as he always did with the stick, to give the orchestra the beat, and sailed into 'Tobermory'.

Success. Within a day offers flooded in and Lauder — grasping at security now; whatever happened he wouldn't go down the mine again — signed himself away to various theatre managers for a total of three hundred weeks, at £10 a week.

Soon he was to regret this — but he carried out each one of the engagements at the agreed fee, even though he requested a few of the dates be altered a bit to allow him to fit in others at ten or fifteen times the rate.

Not too far distant was the time when he would be making £1,000 a week. Perhaps he suspected this — but there was no time to lose. New songs had to be composed — 'Stop Yer Ticklin', Jock', 'Roamin' in the Gloamin'', 'I Love a Lassie', and, of course, 'Keep Right on Till the End of the Road', which has probably given rise to more heartfelt emotion than anything Burns — or Beethoven — ever wrote.

On to America, sailing from Liverpool on the old *Lucania* at the end of 1907, with his son, John, now sixteen. A disastrous press conference; a suddenly truculent and suspicious Scotsman descending a foreign, seemingly hostile gangway; but it was completely forgotten in the thundering success of that first-night success at the theatre in Times Square.

An unbroken tale of success from here on. Tours over much of the world, to whom this little man with the creaking, emotional voice, the infectious — epidemic — laugh, the easily-understood way of speaking and singing, was symbol of all that was best in Scotland. And in a way it was, for this was professionalism at its zenith, with even the manic laugh in 'Stop Yer Ticklin', Jock' being rehearsed daily for ten weeks, every gesture worked out, refined, so that any audience anywhere could instantly be made prisoner. Every community he performed to dredged up its Scots ancestry, found a tartan. There were Scotch Finkelbaums, Scotch di Maggioes, Scotch Joneses, all suddenly awash with haggis, chappit tatties and sentiment: every night was Burns night.

It can't go on — but it does. The years rush by, with ever-increasing success. War comes, and with it personal tragedy: John, the Lauders' only son, a captain in the Argyll and Sutherland, is killed, and the news arrives in London, where he is starring in the revue 'Three Cheers', on New Year's Day 1917. He is heartbroken, considers giving up his career altogether, but is persuaded not to. Visits to the front to entertain the troops, and in 1919 a knighthood.

Much of the rest of Lauder's working life was spent in America or touring the world and, long before the end, these tours were announced, in all sincerity, as 'The Farewell Appearance of Harry Lauder'. But the storms of protest, the urge to keep going anyway, made these farewell appearances an annual affair.

But at last the time came to settle down. He was alone now — his wife had died — and he settled into his large home in Lanarkshire. An earlier attempt to settle at another spot, to be a farming laird, had ended in financial disaster, but here he was happy.

Sir Harry lived until 1950 when he died after the busiest of long lives. — And now, whatever lights — whether they be reed-and-fite-and-blue, or just feeble — may burst over the horizon of the entertainment world, there can never be another Harry Lauder.

Mary Garden

She was vain and often petty. Perhaps it would be fairer just to say she was very feminine.

And she sang like an angel — but more than that: Debussy, Charpentier and others less renowned, swooned when she came on stage.

She came from Aberdeen.

She is commonly believed to have given its name to the gardenia, but as that attractive plant has been around for many, many years, it seems more likely that she gave her name only to a gardenia perfume — and we know she did this.

Her sudden, instant rise to fame, her Cinderella-night, must have been one of the great moments of musical history. The year was 1900, the scene Paris, and the *Opéra Comique*. Gustave Charpentier's opera *Louise*, with some of the most moving,

159

melodious music ever sung, had opened two months earlier. Among the audience tonight was a young Scots girl, Mary Garden, studying to be a singer. She had had the good fortune to be allowed to sing before Albert Carré, Director of the *Opéra-Comique*, had begged a copy of the *Louise* score from him.

And on today, Friday, 13 April, two months after the opera began, she got an urgent message from him: 'Come now and see me.'

She did, tearing down the five flights of stairs like a mad thing, up the street like a greyhound.

There he was. What did Monsieur the Director want?

'I want you to be prepared to sing *Louise*.'

'But — but —'

'You have been studying it — my score — haven't you?'

'Yes, Monsieur Carré —'

Then, going to his desk and taking out a theatre ticket — 'Please sit there, tonight, in the audience. And if Mlle Rioton is taken ill — you take over her part. The lead, Mlle Garden.'

And so she did. The star got through the first two acts, and then, during the second interval, a messenger came to Mary's seat, Number 113, and led her backstage.

She would sing the role: Mlle Rioton had left, plunged out into the street with hysterics, and there was no understudy.

Feverishly, they pinned her into some sort of costume. Not the right one, for there was nothing of the sort that would fit, but a long, blue dress that could be tucked into place around a tiny, seven-stone girl.

The conductor, André Messager — who nevertheless would soon be professing violent love for her — was incensed that his orchestra's performance be made a vehicle for this untried nonentity. It would be better, far better, to give the audience back its money and cancel the rest of the opera.

Carré refused to listen, and the third act began. Mary was led to her spot in the wings and from there she began to study the audience. Everyone was so beautifully dressed: the men, with light glinting off their stiff white shirt-fronts, looked like penguins.

And then she came on. Slowly she walked up to the spot on the stage where she was to sing her aria, *"Depuis le Jour"* — and she sang it.

At the end, André Messager rapped loudly with his baton, made his orchestra stand up and bow to her. The audience thundered its applause, minute after minute.

From then on she sang *Louise* every night. "I began my career at the top, I stayed at the top, and I left at the top. When, many years later, the time came to leave it all, I did so without any hesitation.'

No false modesty about that. And absolutely, exasperatingly, true. It was the secret of the Cinderella success, of the girl who took over the star's part and succeeded. 'I have never been nervous in all my life and I have no patience with people who are. If you know what you're going to do, you have no reason to be nervous.'

Many singers, most of the best ones, might disagree with her. But for Mary Garden it was true.

How did this diminutive Aberdonian find herself in Paris?

She was born, of quite prosperous parents, in 1874. Not 1877, as she let it be known. When she died, on Tuesday, 3 January, 1967, she was just short of her *ninety-third* birthday, and more active than many of us half her age. Her first contact with music, apart from the nursery rhymes she sang with her sisters, was when her parents took her to the Aberdeen Music Hall to hear a statuesque and rather terrifying woman sing *'Ocean, thou Mighty Monster'*. It was thrilling — and the seed was sown.

Mr Garden was offered a better job in America, and accepted. He went ahead, then sent for the rest of the family. Mrs Garden, Mary, Agnes and Amy set sail on the *Anchoria*.

Their first address in a strange land was President Street, Brooklyn. A little later they had moved with father's job to Chicopee, Massachusetts, where a fourth daughter was born. And it was in this town that Mary had a first chance to sing in public. There was a church fête, and during it she was ushered to the front of a platform and asked to perform: someone had heard that Mrs Garden's little girl Mary could sing.

The song, with simpler melody, easier sentiment, than *'Depuis le Jour'* (which had yet to be written) was, *'The Birds Were Singing in Every Tree, at Five o'Clock in the Morning'*.

Great success. And now a musical career, not necessarily as a singer, began to beckon. She took violin lessons.

They returned for a visit to Scotland and Aberdeen. Mary began the piano, worked hard at it, largely because she was in love with Mr Smith. Mr Smith taught the piano in Aberdeen. He didn't know, didn't care, that his protégée loved him — but his physical presence hastened study, and soon she became a skilled performer. The skill would be invaluable to her later, when she began to learn operatic roles.

Back again in America, this time to Chicago, where Mr Garden had transferred to the Pope Company which made bicycles. It was a friendly company under the benevolent rule of old Colonel Pope; and when the boss came to dinner and the meal had been success-fully ended, he turned to Mary, asked her to sing.

She did — and a few days later, at the Colonel's insistence, she had been bundled off to a teacher. Mrs Duff was astounded at the Scots girl's voice, eagerly took her on. Some months later she made the startling request that she be allowed to take Mary to Paris, arrange for her to study there.

What did one use for money?

Mrs Duff would arrange that. She knew rich people, people who would be eager to have a stake in a new, exciting talent. She would get all the backing they needed.

She did, and a little later we find the two of them sailing bravely into the unknown, at the same moment that the Garden family moves yet again, to Connecticut.

Mrs Duff stayed long enough in Paris to find lodgings and a teacher for her pupil, then sailed home. Mary would stay with the Chaigneau family, musicians all, and she would study with one Trapadello.

The singing, and the French, progressed steadily, and after eighteen months had passed our young singer was wondering what chance there was of professional work, however humble. And then, disaster struck. Or so, at the time, it seemed. Her American sponsor refused to go on sending money. No reason was given; it just stopped. And by now she was studying under two teachers, Trapadello and Fugere.

Shaken, she went to each in turn, announced she would be giving up lessons: she had no more money. And both teachers, without hesitation, insisted they carry on, without payment.

Both of these, as in all good fairy-tales, would live to have their gesture rewarded. But an odd, un-fairylike note now intrudes. Mary did everything she could to find why the money had stopped. Free lessons or no, she could not continue indefinitely, even with the sums of money her father now sent, could not go on paying the landlady. But she refused to grovel. When it became clear the money had been stopped deliberately, that there was no question of a mistake, she wrote firmly and told her erstwhile sponsors they could keep the money. Some day she would repay all she'd already had.

The tale is no longer Cinderella's: real human emotions are involved. And in no time at all these are roused to a pitch of rage when a messenger, a woman, arrives from the Chicago sponsors.

'"We have been hearing stories about you —'

'"What sort of stories?" I asked, beginning to sense something ugly.

'"About your private life."

'"Please go on," I said coldly.

'"We have been getting anonymous letters about what you are doing in Paris."

'"And what have I been doing in Paris?"

'"Just about everything — except work."

'"Will you be more specific, please?"

'"They said you had a lover."

'"So that's it," I flung at her. "You can see for yourself the way I am living. Does it look to you as if I have lovers, or that I am not serious about my work?"

'"Also, that you've had a child —"'

So *this* Cinderella has her troubles.

We have no reason to doubt the letters were false, and inspired by jealousy — or straightforward dislike. For here was a girl who was going to get on, and it must have been obvious not only to Mary, but to all who met her. The happy accident over *Louise* would accelerate the process, make possible the boast. 'I started at the top

—', but if ever anything in the arts were inevitable — but, of course, nothing is — Mary Garden was booked for stardom the moment her first teacher heard her sing.

Coupled with talent, a Scots urge to succeed, was a gift for friendship. Men and women simply fell in love with her (though not all of them) and it is easy to see how this would trigger off an avalanche of anonymous letters. Within weeks of losing one sponsor's support she had another, far better. Singers are not as a rule overkind to singers, particularly of the same sex, but an American one was a splendid exception. She was assured and successful, and when she recognized the young Scots girl in the street she invited her into her carriage. What was the reason for that woe-begone look?

By the end of the day the outstanding rent on Mary's lodging had been settled, and she had moved, complete with piano, to a room in the kind lady's house.

And it was there that she met Albert Carré. He told her he was producing a new opera, loaned her a copy of the score. When he found time he even heard her sing. So perhaps it is less than surprising that a waif of a girl — ninety-eight pounds all up — the epitome of all sad little *midinettes* in Paris, who also interested herself in the score of a new opera about a *midinette*; less than surprising that Mary Garden should find herself singing the lead role in *Louise*.

From now on her future was assured. But there were storms ahead. The composer Debussy became hypnotized by her voice — strangely so, because he first heard it in *Louise*, an opera which to the end of his life he loathed. He had collaborated with the writer, Maurice Maeterlinck, over a new and unusual opera, *Pelleas & Melisande*. Maeterlinck wanted his own wife, Georgette Leblanc, to sing the part of Melisande, and according to Mlle Leblanc, writing years afterward about the affair, Debussy agreed that she would.

Rehearsals began. And it was only as Maeterlinck scanned his *Figaro* paper, weeks later, that he saw Debussy had signed up Mary Garden for the part.

Was it true? It was. Was it legal? It was. The law gave no

protection to the author of an opera; the composer had the last word.

Maeterlinck — if we are to believe his wife — then dashed round to Debussy's house, brandishing a cane. Debussy collapsed, was revived by smelling salts, and his wife implored the stick-toting Maeterlinck to go home. And the writer 'who did not like musicians any more than music' laughed and did so.

Perhaps that last sentence from Mlle Leblanc gives us the clue.

Mary Garden's story is a little different. The *Opéra-Comique* had taken the opera under its wing, and the director, Carré, handed out parts himself. One afternoon all the chosen were assembled in a rehearsal room while the composer played and sang the opera to them, from start to finish. A few days later, individual singers were sent one by one into a smaller room at *Opéra-Comique* to sing their parts to Debussy. So far there has been no suggestion that the roles as handed out by Carré met with Debussy's disapproval, no hint that he has someone else (like Georgette Leblanc) in mind. And at the end of Mary Garden's rendition of Melisande — to which he sings Pelleas in a thin, reedy voice — he suddenly gets up, leaves the room.

Puzzled, distressed, she is preparing to leave the building, when she is summoned to the Director's office. She enters, and Debussy gets up from a chair.

'"Where were you born?" he asked.

'"Aberdeen, Scotland."

'"To think that you had to come from the cold far north to create my Melisande — because that's what you're going to do, Mademoiselle."

'Then he turned to M. Carré, and I remember he put his hands up and said, "*Je n'ai rien a lui dire*." "I have nothing to tell her".'

But complications lay ahead. Maeterlinck wrote a bitter letter to the paper *Figaro*, pointing out that not only had 'they' imposed upon him a singer he did not want, but 'arbitrary and absurd cuts' had made nonsense of his story. He ended bitterly with, 'I can only wish for its immediate and decided failure.'

Somebody — perhaps Maeterlinck — printed a programme, with obscene drawings purporting to clarify the misty plot of this impressionist opera. On the night of the dress rehearsal these were distributed among the audience. It rocked with laughter throughout most of the opera, including a death scene over which Debussy had lavished so much care.

The first night, however, went well, but now even Debussy began to have doubts about his work. He explained these by noting that as soon as a composer's work is on the stage, 'nothing remains of the old dream'.

But he had no fault to pick with the young girl who sang it. 'Here indeed was the gentle voice I had heard in my inmost soul, with its faltering tenderness, the captivating charm which I had hardly dared to hope for.'

And Lalo, severest of all French critics, wrote, 'She is Melisande herself'.

For eight years Mary Garden held Paris in the palm of her little hand. Debussy wrote one of his loveliest songs for her, *Extase*, while adding that in any case he had written a whole opera for her before he realized the fact. The American impressario Oscar Hammerstein came over and heard her. He insisted she sign a four-year contract with him. On the understanding that he bring over the entire *Opéra-Comique* company as well, for a season, she agreed.

Her New York début, as it happened, was not a success. It was in 1907, and with the opera *Thaïs*. The critics hated the opera so much that they had few kind words for its star. To someone who had been the darling of a sophisticated audience three thousand miles away, the urge to get up, fly back to Paris, must have been overwhelming. But Mary Garden resisted. The public ignored the critics, began to flock in.

Louise came six weeks later. This time her success was as great as it had been eight years before, when the role of that little *midinette* launched her to fame.

A virtually unbroken success of twenty years followed, in America. The Scots girl seized the heart and imagination of the country, as she had in France. Wherever she sang, houses sold out long in advance.

Not that she didn't occasionally have to fight. On one of these

occasions Hammerstein got the idea of booking the Italian singer
Lina Cavalieri for *Thaïs* in the Manhattan Opera House. Mary was
wild with anger, swore that if Cavalieri sang the role on Friday, she,
Mary Garden, would be on a ship to France by Saturday. She
bought her ticket, waved it.

Hammerstein backed down. And here, in Mary Garden's own
words, is the footnote: 'Cavalieri finally made her début with us in
Carmen. I was in the front box, and my, was it awful! She wasn't
Carmen at all. Hammerstein never gave her the role again. Then she
was given *Tales of Hoffman* to do, and in that she was radiant, full
of diamonds and beauty. After that season she never sang for
Hammerstein again.'

There's always room at the top and Mary Garden deserved her
place: but it's a tough life at that altitude. Perhaps when she decided
to leave, still at the top, and go back to Aberdeen, she felt an inward
relief.

What was she really like, as a singer?

Sadly she made very few records, and those long ago. But they are
absolutely thrilling, even one I have heard which goes back to the
very beginnings of sound recording, long before an electrical system
was invented. She is singing Melisande — and Debussy himself is at
the piano. Another of her rare recordings was made in 1912 — also
before the electrical system — but the high D in that *'Depuis le
Jour'* is liquid — and thrilling. She recorded the same aria years
later, in 1926: now, because she was fifty-two (and not the forty-
nine she claimed) she transposed it down a tone, so that the feat is
less acrobatic, but with the higher standard of recording, more
satisfying to the listener.

She was a very great singer. But her reputation, paradoxically, has
suffered because she was, at the same time, a superb actress. And
opera singers who can really act may be counted on the black notes
of the key of C. Her misfortune, then, has been to be remembered
in some quarters as a singing actress, rather than a singer. But this
would not have upset Mary Garden: either one got under the skin
of the part, lived it as wholly and utterly as any present-day Method
actor — or one did something else for a living.

Her farewell season was with her beloved *Opéra-Comique*, in

1934, when she was sixty. As she had always maintained she would, she retired at the top of her profession. She never gave up her love of singing throughout the more than thirty years of life which remained. To the end she was an encouragement to younger singers, to whom she gave unsparingly of her time — and, on occasion, the rasp of her tongue.

One of those who was helped tells me she remembers Mary Garden, aged eighty, as kind, with a wonderful, ready smile — 'and a loud, *very loud*, speaking voice'. She wore, as she always did, a huge and startling hat, and every move was a picture of grace, theatricality.

The Singing Actress with the thrilling voice died in 1967 still unmarried at the House of Daviot Nursing Home in Aberdeen. She was almost ninety-three.

John Buchan, 1st Baron Tweedsmuir of Elsfield

Two Scottish authors have given me more joy than most writers. One of my two I am forced to leave out, in a book of this size: Mr Eric Linklater started me reading books at the age of nineteen.

Not that I hadn't read before. But somehow, the experience of moving, as a fifteen-year-old adolescent, from one country to another, for keeps, had submerged all desire to read. I put down a book in Boston, Massachusettes, *en route* to catch the boat to England; I never read another — for pleasure, that is — until the age of twenty. Then, in an orgy of delight and discovery, I read everything Mr Linklater had written.

Linklater, alas, did not keep up with my consumption, and I was forced to keep up the habit by reading the work of other folk.

And what was I reading before this self-imposed embargo on the written word?

Needless to say — or we would not have mentioned it here — the tales of Mr Buchan. And Buchan runs neck and neck with Linklater, not in a sober estimate of their worth, which I am not qualified to give, but for the sheer joy they gave me at the time. I was extremely fortunate as a Little-Scotch-Boy at school in America to have the wisest, most understanding of English masters, who led our reading with a gift of insight, so that one was taken from *Twelfth Night* to the *Forsyte Saga* via the enchanting cat Mehitabel and her over-worked amanuensis Archie, who bounced out her blank verse for her each night on Mr Don Marquis's typewriter. Never, of course, using capitals; for though a cat may look at a king, no cockroach can hold down a shift key while he jumps on a letter.

And, of course, this rich and nutritious diet included the red meat of John Buchan. At the time, no bard or cockroach could hold a candle to him.

He was, as it happened, a name well-remembered at my American school. His name is there — somewhere, I remember it clearly — in large letters which proclaim that he gave the Alumni War Memorial Address in 1924. The War Memorial Foundation was intended to provide lectures by the great to inspire the young: it did, and I think still does. Great men were somehow persuaded to travel great distances in order to give the annual talk. Franklin Roosevelt, battling with the cruel paralysis which had seemed to nip off a political career in the bud, came and gave it two years later, in 1926. And others as famous, or about to become so.

But it was not because of the name on the wall that I read John Buchan. I had been interested in him as a fellow Scot and I knew all about him, as people so often do, long before I'd read a line of his work. It was not until I came to *The Thirty-Nine Steps* (fell deliriously, joyously to the bottom) that I was hooked.

He was a man of many parts. Who among us has read his *The Law Relating to the Taxation of Foreign Income?* Not I, but in its day, and perhaps now, it was the definitive text-book on the subject. There is no space here to outline the plot of any of Buchan's books (even *The Law Relating* -), but if by this short re-

telling of his life one person is persuaded to go out and borrow
something of his from the library, something will have been
achieved.

Like Byron — but only in this way, for two men could scarcely
have been less alike — he was a brilliantly gifted amateur, and
regarded himself as an amateur all his life. This, of course, is meant
in the sense of being a lover of many things; for there was not one of
them that Buchan did in an amateurish way. Everything he touched
he did well. And he touched many, many things.

Apart from the tax book which was a succinct and superb setting
out of dismal facts, not intended to bear any relationship with
literature, he wrote on two quite different levels. On one shelf of his
bookcase were his scholarly, readable biographical and historical
works; on another, the rumbustious, blood-and-thunder tales of
adventure. But despite the size of both shelves — and his output
was enormous — he never regarded himself as a professional writer.

What was he then? For this sort of amateur approach quite
understandably sends Americans, Germans and others stark, star-
ing mad. There are, they shout, too many amateurs: captains of
industry who play at being farmers and neither captain nor farm;
non-writing writers; and so on. Yet everything Buchan put his hand
to throve.

A superhuman? No — a very human human. He worshipped
success, enjoyed snobbery and caused endless mirth among his
friends — and enemies — by attempting to be on first-name terms
with everyone from the butler to the Cabinet minister. The late
John Strachey told with a smile how the only person in his life who
had ever addressed him as Jack — and unfailingly did — was
Buchan.

He was born in Perth on 26 August, 1875, the eldest son of the
Rev. John Buchan, whose father before him, and also a John
Buchan, had combined the offices of lawyer and bank manager in
the town of Peebles. The second John Buchan was ordained to the
ministry of the Free Church of Scotland, and it was while he was in
charge of the Knox Church in Perth that his wife gave birth to her
first child, the third John Buchan, and subject of this article.

Before the infant was a year old the family had moved to the manse of the Free Church in Fife, near Kirkcaldy. It was there, four years later, that the future author had an experience which may subconsciously have influenced his choice of the adventure story as chief medium of expression: he fell from a carriage and one of the rear wheels went over his head, fracturing his skull. Yet, always seeing the best in life, he maintained to the end that the long months in bed which followed this so nearly fatal accident permanently improved his health.

Yet in fact it endowed him with a fierce scar and permanently damaged eyesight.

He was thirteen and the family moved again. This time it was the Gorbals, and the manse of the John Knox Free Church — a very different surround to the one at Pathhead. To Sassenachs who believe all Scotsmen talk more or less the same way, it may be hard to realize that the teenage Buchan had difficulty in understanding the Glasgow lilt and in turn being understood himself.

But life was pleasant for the children — there were now four others, all younger than John — and no one objected too strongly when they gave wicked imitations at the dinner table. Imitations of visiting preachers — or even of the old man who made a point of visiting religious meetings, one after the other, and listening politely to confessions of sin. He would then stand up to admit that he, too, would have liked to oblige with a similar recital. Alas, modesty compelled hm to admit that his own life for the past few years had been 'humanly speaking pairfect'.

From this stimulating good-humoured home John Buchan went to Glasgow University. It had only recently moved from its ancient home in the old High Street to its present western one near Kelvingrove Park. He had developed a taste for literature, and with it, a considerable ability at fashioning it himself. Already, at the age of nineteen, he had persuaded a London publisher to let him edit an edition of Bacon's essays. He enjoyed the work, but made no bones about the fact that he was doing it because he needed the money. Like Dr Johnson, he believed no honest man writes a book except to make money.

From Glasgow he was able to get a scholarship to Oxford. By this time he was doing a great deal of writing — simply, he admitted, because he needed a great deal of money. Certainly he could never have got himself through that University, even with his scholarship, without profit from his pen. It goes without saying that the Reverend John Buchan and his wife were far from well off, unable to do much to help their son financially — though they had given him what was far more important; a liberal, and moral, upbringing in a highly intelligent family. (This had even included the chance for young John to take Sunday School classes of his own and entertain the younger generation of the Gorbals by his own, highly dramatized versions of Old Testament adventure.)

In the summer of 1899 he got a First in Greats at Brasenose — and failed to get a Fellowship to All Souls. The next best thing for a young man with his abilities and needs was to become a barrister. (For Scots, the law and medicine have always ranked highest as careers.)

He established himself in London, in the Temple, and subsequently in 1901 was called to the Bar. He was now writing regularly and profitably for the *Spectator*, concealing the fact from his large and rapidly swelling public that they were reading the words of a barrister. He was also writing for *Blackwoods*. He had become a perceptive critic of other men's writing, and approached it with as great an armoury of knowledge, technique and sheer ability as any critic can have mustered in this century. 'Those Who Can, Do: Those Who Can't, Criticize.' Buchan was cheerfully disposing of this old half-truth. He could write in different styles himself, as need or fancy dictated; he knew what made writers tick, could laugh at his own or their foibles. Already, he had made up his mind that he would never be a full-time author. He would always have some other, *serious*, employment, to which he would give the lion's share of his energy. When one considers the vast quantity of literature which he turned out, on several, carefully-surveyed, levels, and the money he made from it, the decision seems hypocritical; but, of course, it was not. Throughout an unbelievably active life Buchan gave himself to his real job, whether it be helping Lord Milner in Africa or being Governor-General of Canada. The sixty-four-dollar question has always seemed to be — how did he find time and mental stamina to write all he did?

Always, from the days of quietly mocking the 'pairfect', John Buchan had hated the bogus, the hypocritical. As a critic he inveighed noisily and happily against The Kailyard School, that peculiarly Scottish manifestation of sentimentality. (The title, for those not familiar with our Scottishisms, comes from the first line of a Jacobite song: 'There grows a bonny brier bush in our kailyard', from which one member of the as-yet-unnamed School had taken a title for his novel. *Beside the Bonnie Brier Bush* he called it, and a great success it was, too). James Barrie must be considered a member of the School: but it extended to other fields, and Harry Lauder, towards the close of his career, was frequently upbraided, because of his dress, his sentimentality, for being a Kailyarder.

As for the self-righteous, particularly in politics, John Buchan had no time at all for them. One well-known Scots politician was thinly disguised in his description of the Home Secretary in a fictitiously awful Liberal Government. The vivid, painful description is in Buchan's *A Lucid Interval*.

But writing this sort of thing for money and fun was all very well: Buchan had to be doing something else. South Africa now swung into focus; the war was drawing to a close and Alfred Milner, as the new High Commissioner out there, had the task of reconstructing the country in a just and enlightened way, particularly the new colonies of the Transvaal and Orange Free State. He wanted, he said, men of brains and character on his staff — and in a hurry. Experience was secondary, for he knew 'first-class men of experience are not to be got, they are too busy already'. Buchan was suggested to him. Very soon the young man was on his way, signed up as Milner's private secretary.

On Buchan's side there was hard-headed realism in this: he gave it much thought before agreeing to go. It was the consideration that he might in the process acquire South African clients for his law practice that convinced him.

Whether he got them is another matter, but he certainly did his work well, and built up, if not an eager clientele, a huge storehouse of experience which was to serve him handsomely in other fields. He admired the Boer fighters immensely, but deplored their 'unlovely kirk', despite a certain similarity to his own. They were, he decided, 'shocking liars' and they used their religion to 'buttress self-sufficiency and mastery over weaker neighbours'. Some years later he was to write *Prester John*, which with all its references to 'blacks' and 'niggers' now offends people all over the world. Yet it is packed with a compassion and real understanding of the black man's dilemma, lacking among some of its critics.

In 1903, his South African work done, he was back in London. Now his energies led him to accept a hard-working directorship with the publishing firm of Nelson. As a barrister he surprisingly dealt with taxation, and it was in this role that he wrote the dauntingly-titled volume on Foreign Income. By this time — though *The Thirty-Nine Steps* was a decade off — he had written much successful fiction on many subjects. He had also produced *The African Colony*, a work of massive scholarship; and — on quite a different level — was mapping out *Prester John*.

He was also missing the open-air life of South Africa. As a substitute, he became enthusiastic about mountain climbing. He tried it in Scotland, tried it in Switzerland, and, though his experience was comparatively limited, was elected to the Alpine Club in 1906, because of his writings on the subject. By now, as we can see, he was a man with a foot in many camps. Not the least of these was the social whirl of London. He complained of the time-wasting necessity of going out, but he went, and in particular enjoyed his country-house weekends. He was beginning to consider a political career — which he would run in tandem with careers as barrister, publisher and writer.

And in 1905 something happened which, though it did not deflect by so much as one degree the purpose of his life to achieve great things in several spheres and become rich in the process, affected it greatly.

Someone took him to dine in London with the rich and well-connected Norman Grosvenors. A little later, he was energetically courting Susan Grosvenor.

He married Susan — on 15 July, 1907 — and as Winston Churchill wrote of his own marriage the following year, 'lived happily ever after'. Susan adapted herself easily to this most un-English of men, even to old Mrs Buchan in Scotland. On their first visits north she understood not a word of what her mother-in-law was saying.

Buchan at the same time was doing well with Nelson's, sending ever larger sums home to his mother and sister, paying for holidays, clothes. He was also doing a lot, in secret, for friends he had made, for descendants of those less fortunate with whom he had worked, for other personal causes.

An example of the energy and ability he poured into everything he did was the Nelson decision to do a Spanish Encyclopedia. Buchan settled down and learnt the language at speed simply in order to edit it. It sold well, became a valuable addition to the Nelson list.

But Nelson's at the time was doing far more than encyclopedias. Under his guidance, they began the famous Nelson Sixpenny Classics, also a Sevenpenny Series of fiction still in copyright, and a Shilling non-fiction series.

The very first of the Sevenpennies, Mrs Humphrey Ward's *The Marriage of the Ashe*, was exhibited a few years ago at the National Library in Edinburgh.

Still restless, anxious to tilt a lance at everything, he became parliamentary candidate for Peebles. He failed to get in. His health, for the first time since the accident with the carriage wheel, had been causing him trouble. His digestion took a disastrous turn from which it never recovered, and he was forced throughout the remainder of his life to adhere — when he could — to a diet.

He was ill when war broke out in 1914. A few weeks later he had his thirty-ninth birthday and began, in bed, writing *The Thirty-Nine Steps*.

He was not recumbent long. His firm decided to do a *History of the War*, written by John Buchan, and would require from him fifty thousand words a fortnight. He settled into this daunting task, and the *History*, published in instalments, was a huge success. All profits from its sale went to war charities.

He finished *The Thirty-Nine Steps*, during another bout of illness, and sent it off to George Blackwood. 'I have amused myself in bed writing a shocker — it has amused me to write, but whether it will amuse you to read is another matter.'

The Times now asked him to visit the front as its correspondent for the Second Battle of Ypres, and he cheerfully accepted. His despatches in the spring of 1915 brought home, as no others did, to the ordinary people of Britain, just what it was like to live in a battle zone. 'In another room is a sewing machine, from which the owner has fled in the middle of a piece of work —' Hardly surprising, then, that this world-renowned war correspondent should have ended the conflict as Director of the Department of Information, the man who perhaps better than any other Briton could tell the world what was happening, and enlist its help. He wrote and wrote, travelled and lectured. He admitted privately that the job was 'the toughest I ever took on'.

But the adventure stories, the thrillers, were coming out now, one a year, sometimes more, and being seized from booksellers by the avid public. They were easy to write, for he based them firmly on the experiences of himself and his friends: the formula, if we may use the term, was to set exciting, often improbably exciting, action against an accurate, factual background. And by this time John Buchan had seen plenty of background, and plenty of action, in South Africa and France.

He was Colonel Buchan now — and suddenly decided he should have a knighthood. His point of view was backed by his mother.

This desire may seem shocking in the eyes of innocents (like me) who have always fondly believed that honours come tumbling, undemanded, down the chimney. But it is only one more facet of the Buchan character. He worshipped success — but it had to be earned. And success should be rewarded. He was disappointed — but not as much as old Mrs Buchan, writing furiously from Scotland — at not receiving the recognition he felt he deserved.

But the urge to be noted, rewarded, did not prevent him from doing what his conscience told him was right. He took the unpopular line of backing conscientious objectors who had been imprisoned for their pacifist beliefs, and fought hard for their release.

Four years ago — and it seemed a lifetime — he had loved Oxford. Now, though his spiritual home would ever be Scotland, he planned to move near that English town. He would have his twentieth-century equivalent of Stevenson's Vailima. He had admired a large house at Elsfield, four miles to the north-east, way back in those undergraduate days, and now he and Susan moved in. He began commuting five days a week to Nelson's in London, and loving it.

His family was growing and — a fact for which some in Scotland have never forgiven him — he sent the boys to Eton. He was proud of his Scotland, stayed there, would always stay there, on every possible holiday occasion, but his mind was not closed to the complementary merits of England, and its way of life, of thinking. No doubt the idea of Eton was Susan's, for all the male members of her family had been there, but he cheerfully agreed to his own boys going there. Though, of course, they would spend school holidays in the north, learning to love it.

So life roared past. The verb may not be quite apposite, but nothing in John Buchan's life moved slowly, however convincing an air he gave of calm deliberation. The thrillers poured out, at least one a year; he wrote incessantly for the weekly press, he wrote historical works. (And re-wrote them, almost in the Soviet Russian sense: he completely re-wrote his *Montrose* in 1928, fifteen years after the original, because of new material and new thinking.)

The honours, at last, began to come. He was Lord High Commissioner to the Assembly of the Church of Scotland in 1933, a particular honour for a son of the manse. It involved residence for a short time in the Palace of Holyrood House, which was not only the chief Scottish residence of the British monarchy but sanctified as the Holy Rood from its connection, hundreds of years before, with Scotland's queen, Saint Margaret.

And in 1927 his urge to enter Parliament was gratified: he became Member for the Scottish Universities.

Eight years later: a far greater distinction. He was raised to the peerage as Baron Tweedsmuir and sent to Canada as Governor-General.

In this role, as indeed in every other he filled throughout one of the twentieth-century's busiest lives, he was highly successful. Popularity is not the sole criterion, but he achieved this and much more besides. Never before had a Governor-General travelled so extensively, got to know his Dominion so minutely. On the other hand, he disappointed Canada's Prime Minister, Mackenzie King: Buchan — or rather, Tweedsmuir — felt himself unable to work with him on the terms of intimacy King had hoped for.

Mackenzie King, though, was one of history's more complex characters, and would deserve a chapter to himself.

Before going to Canada, Tweedsmuir had asked King George V's permission to publish literary work during his term of office. Permission was granted, on the condition that it would not be currently controversial. And so, almost incredibly, in view of the other work he now had to do, more books came from his pen: *The King's Grace*, *The House of the Four Winds*, *The Island of Sheep*, *Augustus* . . .

And, more notable than these, his autobiography, *Memory Hold the Door*, and posthumously, a sad little semi-autobiographical novel, *Sick Heart River*.

He suffered from grave ill-health during these Canadian years, ill-health made worse by his constant travelling, travels which included the United States and an official visit to President Roosevelt. During 1937 he made a journey of *ten thousand miles* into the Arctic and the north of British Columbia.

In the next year, on home leave, he was made Chancellor of Edinburgh University. Perhaps he regarded this as a culmination, the greatest of all his honours.

On 11 February, 1940, while he was shaving — and exactly like Robert Louis Stevenson — he had a stroke and died.

Sixty-four years is not a long life these days. But John Buchan packed into it more than four ordinary mortals could have done in the same time.

Sir Alexander Fleming

He picked up a small piece of mould with his spatula, put it carefully into a test tube. Then he scooped out the rest of the fungus, put that carefully into another.

He had without knowing it taken the first active step towards preparing penicillin. For the moment there was other more pressing work in that laboratory, and he put the test tubes into their rack and got on with it.

But all the while he was thinking, turning over in his mind the implications of what he had seen, what he had done. It had, in a way, been a most ordinary, humdrum occurrence. There were the usual colonies of plump bacteria ripening for examination under the microscope, the usual collection of lab equipment, Bunsen burners, crucibles, pipettes, test tubes. During the day he had taken the lids off several Petri dishes and studied the development of the bacteria within them. Often the bacteria were contaminated by mould — it flew in through the window, or merely spent the day floating about the laboratory, waiting to tumble into an open dish. Then, in no time, the tiny organism, the spore, put out shoots in every direction, grew bigger. It was a nuisance but nothing more: one merely had to dig the thing out and throw it away.

He had found one, been about to clean the dish, when he stopped.

He brought the Petri dish up closer, squinted at it.

Yes — very odd. Very odd indeed. The dish was breeding a colony of staphylococci and the mould, the fungus, had spread from one side and come into contact. But the colony, that part of it which the fungus had spread to, was dead. The staphylococci had been dissolved, and instead of being a yellow clump they had lost their colour, become simply drops of water.

Yes, it had been interesting — and for that reason he had set the mould aside to examine later. To minimize the chance of some mischance, a dirty test tube, a broken one, damaging it, he had divided the thing in two.

And the next day he began to cultivate it. It was still growing slowly when he removed it from the two tubes and spread it on a large bowl of the nutritive broth the lab used for breeding bacteria. Then he covered the bowl with a glass top to prevent further contamination.

The fungus grew, day by day. This, of course, was perfectly natural and it would have been puzzling if anything else had happened. He would just leave it there, let it grow, till there was enough of it to experiment with. Each day he looked in, saw the thick, soft, pock-marked mass change colour from white to green to black, and back again.

Then, without warning, the nutritive broth on which it had been feeding changed suddenly from a clear liquid to a vivid, opaque yellow.

Trembling slightly, Alexander Fleming took a drop of this yellow liquid and placed it carefully at the exact centre of a dish on which he had arranged, like the arms of a star-fish, six different colonies of bacteria, all radiating from the middle. He watched and waited.

Nothing.

And then, to his delight, it happened. Slowly, agonizingly slowly, the streptococci, the staphylococci, the gonococci and the rest of them began to vanish.

This was it. Somehow, he had made a discovery of the very greatest importance. There had been no method at all of killing these bacteria before, only by vicious acids, cruel disinfectants, which would kill the patient as well. Something told him the substance before his eyes was harmless to man, and to prove it to himself he gulped down half a glassful. Then, a trifle apprehensively, he waited for an effect.

None came. The germ-killing substance was harmless to man.

He diluted it, first to a half-and-half solution, then gradually to one part in five hundred. The action was less rapid, but it went on killing bacteria.

The next move was to discover what the substance was — what fungus it had been which found its way into that first Petri dish, a week ago. Frantically he thumbed through books of mycology, the science of fungi, trying to recognize the shape of the growing mould, but to a man, however brilliant, who is not a student of that esoteric branch of science, one mould is much like the next.

But at last, with help, he found it. Penicillium notatum — that was it: a penicillium, or fungus, of the notatum variety. The main problem was to get more of it, for the slow breeding of that original spore would not produce a large enough quantity in a short enough time. He needed the penicillium, and lots of it, right now.

There was another problem. How did one get that yellow liquid into a form stable enough to be stored, to be used when necessary? Already he had seen that the germ-killing quality lasted only a short time before the mould degenerated and turned into an inert, useless liquid.

These two problems were to hold up the development of Fleming's wonder drug for ten years. But as we know, the breakthrough came — and mankind will ever be in Alexander Fleming's debt. The first patient to be treated by the wonder drug, penicillin, was an

Oxford policeman, dying of septicaemia from a small scratch which had infected his blood stream. The date was 20 February, 1941.

There was very, very little of the drug in existence. An intravenous injection was given; another after three hours. At the end of twenty-four hours the improvement was absolutely incredible: the patient had almost recovered, was sitting up, taking notice, laughing.

And then, what Fleming and his helpers had most feared: the penicillin, the whole world's supply, ran out before the treatment was over. The bacteria fought back and slowly got the upper hand. There was nothing to do, nothing at all, but stand by and watch the patient die.

But now the sceptics, or at least many of them, had been convinced. Efforts to produce the stuff in quantity were doubled, re-doubled. It took years — but now there is enough of Fleming's penicillin to treat any man, woman or child in need of it.

Alexander Fleming, son of a hill farmer in Ayr, was born in 1881. There are many Flemings in Scotland and probably the name stems from the weavers and small farmers who fled to England and Scotland from their own Low Countries, at a time of religious persecution. Hugh Fleming, Alexander's father, had an eight-hundred-acre farm called Lockfield, right on the boundary between Ayr and Renfrew and Lanark, though it was just inside Ayrshire. Alec Fleming, subject of this article, was born of his father's second marriage, when the old man was over sixty.

He began going to school when he was five. It was a fine, small, country school, and to the end of his days Fleming maintained that the best, most valuable part of his education had been achieved there, only a mile from Lockfield. Life was pleasant and soon the boy showed an interest in all sorts of sport — an interest which would some day alter the course of his life. He and his brothers, too poor to buy a gun between them, would yet go on rabbiting expeditions through the heather, stalking the little animals, catching them in bare hands. They swam, they ran, they played football, climbed trees: they were happy.

From the little country school Alec Fleming went on to a bigger one in Darvel, the nearest town. This was fun, too, and part of the joy was the walk through the countryside to get there each day, four miles in the morning and four miles back at night. And from the Darvel school to another at Kilmarnock, where the final two years of his schooling took place: he left Kilmarnock, aged fourteen, and headed for London and a job.

The year was 1895, and he was fortunate — as in many ways he remained throughout life. Four of the Fleming brothers had teamed up to rent an old house in the Marylebone Road, and their sister Mary went south to look after the lot of them. Alec's first job was as clerk to a shipping firm and, surprisingly perhaps, he enjoyed the work and might well have stayed on to become an industrial tycoon. But a sudden, unexpected legacy from an uncle made him heed his older brother's advice. 'Don't waste it,' said Tom Fleming. 'Use it to further your education.'

A thoroughly Scottish bit of advice — and Alec took it. A bit of swotting and he sat for the entrance exam. to medical school. He passed and selected St Mary's Hospital in Paddington.

Why did he choose St Mary's? Because he had only recently played water polo against them, thought they were a nice lot of chaps.

And so, as a man of the world who had earned his own living in a quite different field of endeavour and was older than his fellow students Alec Fleming settled down to his studies. We may feel that the years he had spent as shipping clerk were wasted, but Fleming himself said, 'I gained much general knowledge, and when I went to medical school I had a great advantage over my fellow students who were straight from school and had never got away from their books into the school of life'.

At St Mary's he found himself working in the lab of a very great bacteriologist, Sir Almroth Wright.

Why when in fact his bent was for surgery did he change his mind and go on working with Sir Almroth in quite a different field, a field which would have necessitated his leaving St Mary's? Because the great bacteriologist was persuaded to offer the young man the chance of working with him, in order that he stay at St Mary's and support the rifle team.

He passed his finals in 1908, coming top and winning the Gold

Medal of the University of London. He also wrote a thesis on 'Acute Bacterial Infections' and won another medal. The thesis showed the line of research he would follow for the rest of his life. He outlined ammunition at the doctor's disposal in the fight against bacterial disease: there were surgery, when the infection could be reached in that way; antiseptics; general methods of increasing the patient's resistance; the few drugs which had effect on certain specific diseases, like quinine against malaria; ways of increasing the flow of lymph into the infection; and finally serums and vaccines.

An impressive enough list. But something was missing, and it became Alec Fleming's job to find out.

Working in London, he rather surprisingly joined the Chelsea Arts Club, an odd-seeming home-from-home for a country lad from Scotland, but he loved the atmosphere and the conversation, and for the rest of his life this institution remained The Club. He also joined the T.A. — the London Scottish — where there was a chance for sport and a bit of open-air life. His friends were mystified that Fleming, as a trained and unusually well-qualified bacteriologist, should choose to become a private soldier in the Territorial infantry, but Fleming spent several happy years in that friendly avocation, doing his summer camps with six or seven other men sharing a tent. He only left when the training periods began to conflict with his work at the hospital.

A few months after his resignation in 1914, war broke out. He rejoined the army, but now in his proper role, and almost immediately he found himself as a lieutenant in the medical research centre in Boulogne.

Very soon Fleming was forced to re-think his thesis on bacterial infection. Wounded men, dying men, were brought in on stretchers, their wounds crawling with bacteria, and he found out only too soon that his antiseptics were useless. Not only did they not prevent, for example, gangrene: they actually seemed to promote its development. If a wound were near the surface the antiseptic could be useful, for a strong enough dose of it would indeed kill germs — and all the surrounding tissue at the same time. For a surface wound, some types of surface wound, this was acceptable. But, of course, most wounds were the reverse of superficial and here the antiseptics were either useless or destroyed vital tissue, or somehow destroyed the body's ability to fight back.

He realized that only one sort of antiseptic would be of real value — and that hadn't been discovered. A substance which would help the body's natural defences, that was the only solution.

For years he would search for that substance.

The war ended and Fleming went back to civilian research, with an eye open for his wonder drug. He felt it might have to be something from the body itself, and in 1921, after three years of research into the matter, he found that human tears had a startling effect on bacteria. If one dropped them into a culture, they dissolved the germs as if by magic. He analysed the tear drop, found it contained a substance which he christened lysozyme and which he isolated in hair, skin, nail-parings and certain leaves. It seemed a dramatic discovery.

Then he found that lysozyme, though dramatically effective against certain bacteria, was almost useless against any of the dangerous ones. He had come up against a wall — but it would not discourage him.

Eight years went by, from 1921 to 1929, and Fleming worked ceaselessly on the theory that something from the human body would be the answer to bacterial infection. Lysozyme was no good — but it had pointed the way.

And then, in 1929, through the window of his laboratory in St Mary's Hospital, Paddington, the answer literally blew in. The fungus, penicillium notatum, fluttered down and settled in Alexander Fleming's Petri dish of cultures.

As we have seen, it provided the answer. It might not be a substance from the human body, but it occurred naturally and it dramatically inhibited the growth of micro-organisms. How, though, did one get enough of it, and stabilize it so that it could be stored, used when wanted?

Fleming had the patience of Job. For, having struggled eight years to get from lysozyme to penicillin (he coined both names himself), he was to labour another twelve before penicillin could be stabilized. Even then the quantities made available were minute. It was at this point, in February, 1941, that treatment was carried out on the Oxford policeman, treatment which ended in personal tragedy, but marked a further step in the development of the drug.

By this time the Australian Howard Florey had become interested in the work and assembled about himself a team of able chemists. They found, after months of frustrating work, that they were able to purify small quantities of the mould by a complicated method of evaporation — freeze-drying — and in this condition it could be stored for a short time. But, of course, far greater quantities had to be made, and a new source of the mould had to be found, for Fleming's original two test tubes of the notatum just wouldn't yield enough. To this end help was sought in America, and at last a laboratory in Peoria, Illinois, came to the rescue. The lab had been working on uses for the organic by-products of farming, and although they had not obtained any of Fleming's mould in the course of their work, they had discovered that cornsteep liquor, made from maize, was an ideal medium for the growth of fungi — far better than the usual broth that chemists used. Some of Fleming's original fungus was accordingly rushed to the United States where it began proliferating.

At the same time the research team, in England and America, was on the look-out for mould-strains which might give a bigger yield of penicillin. All of it now in existence had descended from the spore that landed on Fleming's bench in 1929.

Then, in 1943, another break-through. The Peoria lab was already, thanks to its corn-steep liquor, producing twenty times as much as Howard Florey's team in Oxford. And one of its employees, a young woman employed to go round the markets of Illinois looking for rotten fruit, brought back a melon. It was in a splendid state of decay, and the usual tests on it produced the welcome discovery that its penicillium chrysogenum provided a mould of the penicillin type, which reproduced itself at great speed.

Success at last, and with it a realization by scientists in England and America that a wonder-drug was in reach. Production mounted rapidly in both countries, and with it, technique for stabilizing the product. At first almost all of the penicillin was earmarked for the Services, and during the next two years thousands of lives would be saved on the battlefields by it.

By the end of the war enough could be made available for civilian patients as well. And now honours began to shower down on the shy and sensitive Alexander Fleming. He had already been knighted — in the basement of Buckingham Palace — during 1944. He had received the freedom of Paddington, the home of St Mary's, where he had made the discovery; had received, too, the freedom of the little Scots town of Darvel where he had been at school. Now, in 1945, he was invited to the United States, to be fêted, and at the same time see how his brain-child was being developed, produced, in ever increasing quantity.

He was delighted to find that none of the firms — in America or in Britain — which were manufacturing the drug were making an attempt at monopoly. He had set the example himself by refusing to patent it, thereby passing up the opportunity of becoming a very rich man, and now the manufacture of penicillin, as he had long hoped, was public property. All firms, all research teams, shared their knowledge.

At the end of that triumphant year Alexander Fleming learnt he had been awarded the Nobel Prize for Medicine.

There was sadness ahead: throughout the long and lonely years in which Fleming had battled to make penicillin and to interest others in trying to help him, he had been wonderfully buoyed up by his wife, Sareen. She had been his constant companion for thirty-four years. When she died, in October, 1949, he was heartbroken. The tragedy was heightened by the fact that penicillin could do nothing for her — and by the sad remembrance of his brother's death, which penicillin, had he been able to use it in those days, would have averted.

To one of his oldest friends, he said, 'My life is broken'. Work was his only refuge and he plunged into it, devoting day and night, his entire life, to research. One of his team was a brilliant young Greek biologist, Amalia Voureka, who had received a British Council bursary, and been working in Fleming's laboratory since 1946. He had admired her work, begun to feel an affection for her, and in April, 1953, four years after the death of his wife, he married Amalia Voureka.

Their happiness was to be short-lived. He was an old man now. and illness struck at him frequently. On one occasion he diagnosed his high temperature as pneumonia, the disease which had killed his brother John. He sent for the doctor, who confirmed that it was, and immediately injected penicillin. The improvement was so sudden and so marked that Fleming laughed like a child and said, 'I never knew it was so good!' But his health failed gradually, and in 1955 he died of a disease his drug was powerless to control, coronary thrombosis.

There can have been few great men so modest and few who did more for mankind. It may be argued in a decade or two from now that Alexander Fleming, by saving so many millions of lives and ensuring the survival of millions more down our succeeding generations, has, alone, created the population explosion which will ultimately destroy us.

But if it does, we have only ourselves to blame.

No one who has seen a friend or dear one brought back from the very brink of death by one of the antibiotics which Fleming's penicillin triggered off, could feel that the shy, retiring Scotsman was anything but one of the greatest men the world has ever known.

John Logie Baird

In May, 1941, the BBC organ *Radio Times* ran an article on television. 'A week or two ago, we made a mention of colour television. Now we have seen it for ourselves. John Logie Baird gave us a demonstration of the system on which he is now working; he has been using colour television in one form or another since 1928. He is now using 600 lines, which is very much higher than the standard officially fixed for black-and-white television at Alexandra Palace before the service was closed down by the outbreak of war.'

And now, forty-odd years later, how much farther have we got?

But John Logie Baird, inventor-by-necessity (it was the only job his health would permit, and he set himself to it as another man might become a writer), Baird has received very little credit for the fact that he showed the world's first colour television. And — far more important — that he showed the first moving television picture of any sort.

He was — obviously — a remarkable man. Without him, television, though it might exist in a practical form today, would almost certainly be less developed, less efficient. He gave it a head-start, for like Marconi he was able to sift out the ideas of other men, improve and expand them into something remarkable and worthwhile.

Unfortunately for Baird, his mind, his inventor's, innovator's, mind was far too active. Stages in the development of his telly brainchild (and no one west of the Iron Curtain is likely to deny him paternity) which he should have followed up himself, or at least kept under the closest personal control, were often left to subordinates, while the brilliant J.L. Baird rushed on with newer, better ideas. We do not know which of these it was that the *Radio Times* raved over in 1941, but a year previous to that Baird himself described his new 'Deluxe Superscreen Teleradiogram'. It showed a picture two feet six inches square, and was fitted with push-buttons. These brought into action an all-wave radio set; an automatic record-changing gramophone, the BBC Television Programme, the 'Baird Colour Television Programme' *and* the 'Baird Stereoscopic Television Programme'. Had Baird settled for a little bit less, like cutting out his Stereoscopic programme, we might well have had colour television in Britain far sooner.

But Baird, though he liked money and what it could buy at least as much as the rest of us, was the least commercial of men. With a lot more business acumen, coupled with a realization that first things, in commerce, come first, he would have died a very rich man. He would almost certainly have become a peer, too. Though I like to think of him as the shy and brilliant Mr Baird, with the short sight which occasioned that first, terrifying meeting with John Reith — on another page — I cannot think of him as Lord Baird of Gogglebox.

He died in 1946 — neither a rich man nor a very famous one. He might have been amused to see how famous he then became.

But back to the beginning. He was born in 1888, and like a surprising number of those in these pages, Reith included, he was a son of the manse. Sometimes that seems almost a first ticket towards fame. His father was minister of the West Parish Church of Helensburgh on the Clyde. Young John seems to have been a normal lad with a slightly precocious interest in technology; with another boy he made a life-size aeroplane, or at least, in his own words, 'a weird contraption, two box kites joined in the centre'. It was only a year or two after the thrilling first exploits of the Wright brothers, and like them John and his friend Godfrey planned to glide first, then attach an engine and really fly.

But here we get an insight into Baird's character; the frankness, the modesty — which gives more than a clue to his failure in later life. For frankness and modesty, as distinct from an appearance of both these attractive attributes, are, sadly, two qualities least wanted in the tough, twentieth-century world of commerce, or most other worlds. Did Baird fly, taking his life in both hands, and of his own free will? Not likely; he'd had no intention of risking his neck, he tells us; that was for young Godfrey. Baird just happened to be on board their wondercraft when 'Godfrey gave the machine one terrific push and I was launched, shouting, into the air. I had a very few nauseating seconds while the machine rocked wildly and then broke in half and deposited me with a terrific bump on the lawn.'

And he never, ever, had any further desire to fly.

From local school to the Royal Technical College, Glasgow. Here, though he worked extremely hard, for he was poor and desperately needed a good job at the far end of the tunnel, he did badly. This was largely owing to the ill-health which dogged him throughout his life — and to which, in a way, we owe television. He eventually completed the course and persuaded his parents to let him use the Associateship of the Technical College he had thus acquired to go and work for a B.Sc. at Glasgow University.

This was 1912. Two years later, the First World War broke out. Urged by a sense of duty and what he described later as 'possibly the desire to appear well in the eyes of my friends', he offered himself to the army and was smartly rejected. The army had no time to waste on someone who was so obviously a candidate for the sick-bay.

He completed his University course and took a job as electrical supply engineer. It was miserable work, rushing out to deal with mains failures and the like, at all hours of the day and night, and his health suffered. But it was a vicious circle, which his boss summed up in a memo: 'We cannot give Baird a better job: he's always ill.'

So he left. Anything must be better than this — and the 'anything' which John Logie Baird chose was to be a professional inventor. He would start by improving and marketing other people's ideas and the first one he selected was a formula for easing the discomfort of haemorrhoids. No doubt it is as well for posterity's legend of John Logie Baird that his cure was a flop and was hastily withdrawn.

But the pattern is emerging.

From pile cures to diamonds, which would be home-made from carbon. His idea, though chemically sound, was another failure, so he rushed on to make and market 'The Baird Undersock'. This would be 'Medicated, Absorbent and Soft, keeping the Feet Warm in Winter and Cool in Summer. Ninepence per pair, Post free.'

After a shaky start (the newspaper advertisement cost thirty shillings and it sold one pair of socks for ninepence), he actually began to make a success of the idea. But once again ill-health struck him down: he suffered so long and so severely from a cold, with the one-man business vanishing behind his back, that he gave it up. When he recovered from the cold he realized it was time for another dramatic interference with his own destiny. He spent all his sock-profit on a one-way ticket to Trinidad. Here at least he would be warm and well.

Like an early explorer, he took with him cases full of trinkets to sell to the natives. We have no space to go into his performance as a businessman in the Caribbean paradise, but we must register that as a trader Baird was a flop. He sold his stock at a thumping loss — and then rushed on, with the same youthful enthusiasm, to start a jam factory.

Here everything possible went wrong: enormous ants stormed in and made off with a hundredweight of sugar overnight; the jam (and the chutney and the syrup and the jelly) filled up with loathsome insects. Small wonder that he had the greatest difficulty in selling any.

Ill-health again and on his recovery he decided to set sail for England, bearing tins of his product, to sell in Britain.

We need not consider what happened. After some more disasters — and one or two very near misses in which he *almost* laid his hands on a fortune — Baird found himself in 1923, aged thirty-five, in Hastings, on the south coast. Here, even without much money, he would have fresh air and sunlight. And here he would settle down and really be an inventor, not just a marketer of other people's ideas.

He sat down and started inventing.

Glass razor-blades were among the earliest of his inventions. They were a disastrous precursor of today's blades of stainless steel, and they were quickly followed up by pneumatic shoes like car tyres and intended for the same purpose, to give a smooth ride; but they had the unfortunate result of making the pedestrian seem very drunk indeed.

And then suddenly he remembered an idea which had popped in and out of his fertile mind many times since childhood: pictures by radio.

And this — as we now all know — worked. Somehow Baird seems to have known it would, and he put all his energies into this one exciting idea, forgot all about razor-blades and socks and jam: he would send a picture by wire — and soon.

But although Baird made something practical out of it, the idea of sending pictures along wires and even through the air had been in the minds of others for years, ever since Marconi had sent his first radio message. The German Paul Nipkow had produced his Nipkow disc by the time Baird turned his brain to the idea, and this disc was, in its crude way, the forerunner of all television. By punching holes in a certain way round the periphery of a cardboard disc, Nipkow found he could illuminate an object in front of the disc with a light from behind it; illuminate in a series of tiny points of light which scanned the object from top to bottom and from side to side. If this illumination of, say, a human head could be picked up by a light-sensitive device, a photo-electric cell, the consecutive points of light, each of varying intensity depending on the light and shade of each part of the face, could be sent along a wire as separate electric pulses, of different strength. If these pulses could then be converted back into light, through a bulb, and re-constituted by a similar disc, in the right order, flashing the points of light on a screen, the original object — the human head — would be reproduced on it. And if the two discs revolved fast enough, spattered their points of light fast enough to make use of the eyes' natural persistence of vision, the picture would seem complete, not just a series of dots.

Nipkow's apparatus was far too primitive to transmit anything recognizable, but the principle was sound, and it was this that Baird set out to develop. He worked out a plan of scanning so that the dots moved from left to right in horizontal lines, thirty of them, one line below the other, to fill up a frame. (The BBC now uses 625 lines, but in exactly this way.) The frame itself would be swept away to make room for another, many times a second, like successive pictures in a cine film.

Baird put immense concentration into the task: he experimented with different-size discs, with different numbers of holes, different speeds of rotation; and with different photo-electric devices. And at last, to his unspeakable joy, he was able to transmit along a pair or wires, the shadow of a small Maltese cross.

Others had been working along these lines in different parts of the world — but Baird was way out in front.

But now troubles began with Mr Twigg, his landlord in Hastings. Mr Twigg was shocked and alarmed at the dangerous nature of the experiments he believed were being carried on upstairs, and a fierce argument ended in Baird's removal to London. But there is now a plaque mounted on the wall of that little Hastings shop above which Baird had his lab. It reads: 'Television, first demonstrated by John Logie Baird, from experiments started here in 1924.'

These experiments were now continued in an attic at Number 22 Frith Street in Soho, while Baird himself lodged out at Ealing. So far he had little more than the transmission of a small cross to his credit, but he had an absolute faith in himself and knew, somehow, that the rest would follow. But he must have money. He canvassed prominent people and newspapers, most of whom dismissed him as a lunatic. But gradually interest grew, and some rash folk even invested a little money into his invention. He was helped by the enterprise of Gordon Selfridge, who wanted a demonstration of something exciting for his big London shop's Birthday Week. For the princely sum of £20 a week, for three weeks, Baird eagerly demonstrated his toy, and puzzled customers bent down to marvel over silhouettes transmitted a number of yards along a mere piece of flex.

Two far-sighted commercial firms now came to the rescue: one, having failed to sell the penniless inventor £200 worth of batteries, gave them to him; and another gave him valuable valves.

And on a winter's evening in 1925 — break-through:

The evening before, he had run through a whole chain of experiments and tests. He had altered the equipment a dozen times, replaced almost all of it. The only survivor was Bill, the mute, sympathetic witness who had attended every experiment since the transmission, more than a year back, of the Maltese cross. Bill was a dummy.

He sat Bill up in his chair, switched on the apparatus and walked into the next room.

There he tuned in his receiver, got a pink rectangle in the viewing box, focused it. He ran back to the other room, adjusted the light over Bill's head.

Back to the receiver. Now the pink glow was streaked with black bars. There was always a few seconds of this, while receiver and transmitter got into sync. After this, if things went as usual, there would be Bill, just a black-and-white, fuzzy-sided silhouette. Not a picture at all.

Suddenly the picture locked, the bars vanished, and Baird gasped. There Bill was. Bill in his viewing box — but not just a black-and-white outline, a child's drawing: he was there, every feature recognizable, eyebrows thick and curving, head correctly rounded.

Baird tore down the steps to the floor below and burst in on William (whom we must not confuse with Bill), the office boy of the firm downstairs. William was sorting envelopes and he looked up in some surprise as the 'mad Scotch inventor' from upstairs burst in.

In a few moments he had been persuaded to leave the envelopes, and shaking his head he followed Baird up the steps to his lab. A flick of the wrist and the dummy was on the floor, grinning at the ceiling. A moment later William was in his place. 'Sit still — that's all. Sit *still* —' Baird was off.

But this was dreadful. A moment ago there had been a picture. Now there was nothing. He tore back, ready to put the dummy back in his seat, send William back to his envelopes. Then he saw what was wrong.

'I *know* it's hot — but you've got to sit up, just where I put you. Look, here's half a crown —'

Back to the receiver, heart pounding.

And there, in that other room, was the office-boy's face: puzzled, indignant, but there, with every part of his round face clear and in focus, correctly shaded.

And William, this young man whose face was the first ever to be seen on television — and who, a moment later, when they reversed roles, became the second man in history to see television, went back, grumbling, to his envelopes.

So this was it! No need to go back to jam and undersocks now.

He worked harder still, for many weeks. Then, in January 1926, he recklessly issued an invitation to the Royal Institute in London — all of it — urging it to come to a demonstration.

He was shocked at the large number which did so, and they were shocked at the smallness of his premises, but somehow the demonstration was shown to all of them. Bill's face and those of distinguished scientists were transmitted, time and again, from one room to the next.

Baird had demonstrated real television. The next step was to send these visual images over a distance, and now he received welcome help from the Chief Engineer of the BBC (still the infant British Broadcasting Company). They let him send his picture along the telephone wires to a BBC studio and then put it out on the air for him. Baird himself picked it up on a receiver at 22 Frith Street, and was overjoyed to find his picture 'practically unaltered' by what the BBC had done to it.

But he wouldn't be able to use BBC transmitters for ever: they had other things to do; and if he used them after late-night close-down someone would have to pay the staff that manned them. If Baird wanted to go on transmitting television signals into the air he would have to build his own transmitter, and get it licensed.

He did — and 2TV became the first licensed television station — indeed the first television station, licensed or no — in the world. He moved from Frith Street to slightly larger accommodation near Leicester Square, built his transmitter there and received the pictures on receiving apparatus in Harrow, ten miles away.

Flushed with excitement, he rounded up a few partners and formed Television Limited.

It seemed as if the whole world were at his feet. Early in 1928 he transmitted a picture across the Atlantic, and a little later to the liner *Berengaria* in mid-ocean.

But now his luck turned — and Baird's bitter words tell us why:

'If an inventor reads these pages, let him by this be admonished and do what Graham Bell, inventor of the telephone, did, and sell for cash. Inventors are no match for financiers where stocks and shares are concerned, and will, if they hold on, find that the financiers have the cash and they have the paper.'

John Baird made little money out of his invention. Partly through his lack of business ability, partly through bad luck, he found others reaping the benefit of his work. When he died in 1946 he was not the rich man he had hoped to be. It has been said that he 'sold himself to Mammon' too soon; if he had not allowed unsuitable people to take shares in his invention at too early a stage he would have retained greater control over it. He might have convinced John Reith, the daunting head of the BBC, that this was a discovery which needed to be used, and used soon, which wasn't a commercial stunt. As it was, the BBC, after taking years to work up a real interest in television, or agree to any system of transmission, finally settled on another one which had been developed after Baird's and yet which owed its very existence to those early experiments in Hastings and Soho.

He was disappointed, terribly disappointed — but he went right on inventing. Colour TV, stereoscopic TV, large-screen TV, TV-on-your-telephone: all these things Baird worked on, made work.

Yet he died, if not exactly a poor man, a lot less rich than he might have been. In fact, at one stage, a very early stage, he had been offered £125,000 for his shares in his own Baird Television. This he characteristically refused by saying: 'I just wouldn't know what to do with that sort of money; why, I'd not be able to sleep at night.' So he hung on, hacking a way for others.

He died after yet another of the severe bronchial troubles which had plagued him from childhood (the trouble which had driven Alexander Graham Bell from Britain to invent the telephone in America). He was buried near where he had been born, in the little churchyard at Helensburgh, on the Clyde.

Five years went by.

And then, quite suddenly, another plaque in his memory went up. This man who had demonstrated television in black-and-white, in colour, in relief and — at the very end of his life — in the dark (using infra-red rays to transmit a picture of something the human eye could not see), John Logie Baird was acknowledged as the Man who Invented Television.

John Charles Reith, First Baron of Stonehaven

'I met Reith for the first time in rather unfavourable circumstances. I was always very short-sighted, and at the beginning of one of the classes the Professor asked if those who were short-sighted and wanted front seats would hand in their names. When I went up to the platform to hand in my own, three large, impressive young students were talking to him. They were talking on terms of equality. As I did so, the heaviest and most overpowering of the three 'heavies' turned round and boomed at me, 'Ha! What is the matter with you?'

The words are John Logie Baird's, and it would seem that throughout his life poor Baird, inventor of television, was in awe of the enormous fellow-countrymen on whom — or so Baird thought — so much of his future depended.

So much has been said and written about Lord Reith; he was such a part of life in Britain, such a national institution, that while one may not be able to add to the sum of human knowledge on this sometimes controversial subject one cannot omit such a towering twentieth-century personality from a collection of Scottish lives.

The BBC has had a number of chiefs since Reith's day, some of them providing almost as much material for staff humour and 'In' jokes as the First of All. The Reith legends were often built around the presumed piety of the great man, and like all good legends — though this is not to question that piety — they were largely untrue. I suppose my favourite is of the occasion he descended on Broadcasting House late one evening and was taken round the studios. A play was going out, and the Continuity Announcer, who therefore had nothing to do till the end, when he would intone 'That was — ', seemed to have vanished.

Suddenly, to the horror of the middle-man who was conducting his Director-General, the announcer was discovered behind an acoustic screen in the arms of a young woman.

Middleman and Reith — so legend runs — turned around with dignity and left the studio. They walked in terrifying silence for hundreds of yards through the battleship interior of B.H., and then the middle-man turned, pale and trembling, and said to his superior:

'Sorry about that, sir. Very bad show.'

'Indeed, yes. And just who *was* that — er — young man?'

The middle-man told him.

'I see.' Reith turned on his heel. 'Well, he must *neverrr neverrrr* be permitted to read the Epilogue.'

That was years ago. Nowadays reputations crumple more easily, mean less in the first place. Nobody cares, and nobody would bother to make up a story like that. Some time ago I was on the third floor of Broadcasting House, where an inches-thick blue carpet outside the lift signified that one was within yards of the Director-General's office. It was late at night and no one — not even the prowling shade of that first D.G. — was about the passages. The very young man who was with me went up to a handsome bronze bust on a stand just outside the D.G.'s locked door. Of course, it was Reith. Suddenly he stuffed an arm up inside it. There was a sound like a distant dinner gong.

'The Head of Our Founder,' he said with a grin. 'Quite, quite, hollow.'

In fact, no description of John Reith could be less apposite. If ever there was a man who never stopped thinking, or doing, it was Reith.

There are many contradictions about him. One is that he never appeared to give a damn what the other fellow thought, or did, as long as he, Reith did what he felt was right. And in the case of poor Baird, to whom the terrifying meetings and negotiations with the then Director-General of the BBC seemed a matter almost of life and death, the little man seems scarcely to have registered at all. It was decided not to use his method of television transmission: that's all there was to it.

In Reith's fascinating autobiography, *Into the Wind*, there are 236 pages dealing almost exclusively with the BBC from its inception (when he took command) to the day in 1938 that he left. On not one of those pages is Baird mentioned: that name which was a household word when the BBC led the world in TV, in the 'thirties, is not in the index, or anywhere else.

Baird obviously made no impression at all: Reith did what he thought was right.

But within the pages of that autobiography there are a surprising number of testimonials to the author, quoted at length. Things like 'Even those not given to hero-worship can look upon Sir John Reith as one of the few really great men of our time — '; 'By your own efforts you have done more than tongue can tell — '; 'Vehement, determined, aggressive, masterful, capable of thinking and administering on the big scale —'. Example after example of this sort of thing, with the comments, as well, of two British Prime Ministers, Ramsay MacDonald and Stanley Baldwin, about the great difficulties of being Prime Minister. One is quoted as saying to Reith, 'Maybe you'll find out for yourself one day'; the other, on a later occasion, remarks, 'Perhaps *you'll* find that, some day'.

There is also a rather baffling document, quoted in its entirety as a 'Testimonial' from three Glasgow University students, fellow members of the Officers' Training Corps. One of them was O. H. Mavor, soon to become the playwright James Bridie. They testify that Reith is the 'only sergeant in the Corps with the smallest right to pretensions of honour, manliness or good fellowship ... we could go further, but our pen is done'. It is oddly reminiscent of what three other Glasgow University Students had done to 'William McGonagall, Poet and Tragedian', that most ridiculed of all Scots.

So it seems the biographer is left with a man of intelligence, moral fibre, organising ability, refusing to suffer fools gladly or at all — and aware of all this. And probably no other man could have piloted the infant British Broadcasting Company, and the Corporation it became, piloted it through the shoals; could have dealt with little prime ministers, little kings, and got his way. This is no place for a write-up of the BBC, but few would deny that what it is today, from the accepted impartiality of its news to its often outrageous debunking programmes in which no person or institution is safe, it owes in some measure to John Reith. As a Canadian newspaper suggested a while ago during a long article about the excitement for Canadians of short-wave listening: 'Whizz round the dial and hear what's happening, from Washington, from Paris, Moscow, Peking, Bonn. And then, to find out what *really* happened, tune to London.'

The first Baron Reith of Stonehaven could hardly ask for a more suitable scroll on his coat-of-arms.

But enough, for the moment, of the BBC. John Reith was there for rather less than sixteen years. What about the rest of him?

For what he looked like we can do no better than turn to John Logie Baird again. This is Reith, observed during a confrontation over the future of television: 'A large gaunt frame surmounted by a grim, rugged visage, surmounted in turn by a domed forehead, rendered more impressive by a heavy scar.'

He was born in 1889, son of a minister of the Church of Scotland at Stonehaven, on the north east coast. After eight years at Glasgow Academy he was sent for another two to an English public school, Gresham's School, in Norfolk. Thence to Glasgow Technical College, as prelude to what was intended to be a career in engineering. It was at the Tech that the class-room meeting with Baird took place, and as we know that he would have preferred to do almost anything else — preferably academic — than be pushed into engineering, he must have been unhappy at the time. His father had decreed that every man, whatever his inclinations, should learn a trade. At his English public school he had enjoyed being a member of the Corps, had become a sergeant. In Glasgow he kept up his military hobby with the University OTC — where he received his 'Testimonial'. Early in 1914, aged twenty-four, he travelled south to London in search of a job, and got it with Pearson's, the big civil engineers. This was pleasing, up to a point, for he was glad to be out of mechanical engineering, able to deal with bridges, not boiler-rooms.

In 1911 he had been commissioned in the Volunteers — the 5th Scottish Rifles — and on the outbreak of war in 1914 he eagerly reported to them. After the initial confusion of mobilization he was finally settled in as commander of the transport section with the privilege of 'wearing spurs'. And the little phrase has given a title to a delightful book he wrote about that military life.

He was transferred, because of his specialist knowledge and his inclinations, to the Royal Engineers, and it was with them in October, 1915, that he was badly wounded. He made an astonishing recovery from a head wound, demanded to be sent back to the front, but was invalided out of the service.

His senior at Pearson's, E. W. Moir, had been ordered to the United States to organize munitions supply, and now, at Moir's request, young Reith went along as his assistant. The job seems to have involved travelling about American munitions factories and checking on the suitability of what was being manufactured for the British services. He spent eighteen months in America and liked it enormously. Always in later life he welcomed an opportunity to go back.

But he had his reservations about American big business — and these must have considerably influenced him when British broadcasting began.

War ended and he found himself, after some indecision, working as General Manager of a big engineering firm in Scotland —

William Beardmore and Co. It was not what he had in mind as life's work, and in 1922 he resigned.

And it was in October of that year that he saw the advertisement for a General Manager to take charge of the new 'British Broadcasting Company (In Formation)'.

As everyone knows, he got the job, and he literally made the Company. The history of the BBC from Company in 1922 to Corporation in 1927, to its present position in the late 1980s, has already been well documented. We may sum up, if we wish, by saying that Reith, in the course of his fifteen and a half years in broadcasting, created and developed a broadcasting system for the British Isles which was to foreshadow the pattern of publicly owned but independent utility corporations, from the Tennessee Valley Authority to British Airways; he started an Empire broadcasting service on short waves; and he instituted the first regular service in the world of high-definition television — way back in 1936.

Reith fought not only for what he felt was right — and fought like a tiger — but for his employees (which is not always the same thing). He defended them to the hilt in their work; and workers in a monopoly system of broadcasting, completely surrounded by a Press which understandably wants to set up in opposition, with 'a licence to print money', often need defence.

Early in 1936, John Reith cut out and kept a Buckingham Palace announcement of a dinner party at which 'Mr and Mrs Ernest Simpson' had been present. At the end of the year he was making the arrangements for Edward VIII's Abdication Speech.

Those who heard that speech may recall a loud bump near the beginning. Reith, who announced the king himself, was accused of saying his piece and banging the door as he went out. But in fact the noise was caused by the royal knee coming in contact with the table-leg.

He had been knighted in 1927, when the original Company became a Corporation. The peerage, as Lord Reith, was to come thirteen years later, in 1940, some two years after he had left the BBC; so it is as Sir John that he is remembered; the idea of having a Baron-in-charge-of-Broadcasting is tempting and one wonders what the Press might have done with it.

In 1938, with his BBC running smoothly, he felt in need of new worlds to conquer. From a figure of 36,000 wireless licence holders, when he and another three men had set up their embryo Company, to 8,700,000 licences when he decided to leave, the expansion, the progress, had been almost continuous. It would be — and was — a great wrench to leave what he had come to regard as his life's work, but he did it. His description of going down to Droitwich on his last evening, driving in and asking to close down the big oil engines of the high-power transmitter, is moving. On he goes, to Daventry, driving through the night, dawn climbing up into the sky as he gets there; and the red lights on the aerial masts switch off. No need to ask how to deal with the mechanism, for this broadcaster started life dealing with it. 'A new day was breaking for Daventry and the BBC. In it I was nothing and nobody to Daventry and the BBC.'

Perhaps not — but the world would be hearing more from John Reith. He had accepted the post of Chairman of Imperial Airways, an organization badly in need of his help, and a little later he was responsible for its merging with the 'British Airways' of the day to become BOAC.

War came; with it more demand for his services. He became successively Minister of Information, Minister of Transport, Minister of Works and Buildings. The peerage came in 1940 and he chose his tiny East Coast birthplace for the title 1st Baron Reith of Stonehaven. In 1942 — great disappointment. Churchill, with whom he never saw eye-to-eye, dismissed him from his ministry. Determined to keep working 'at full stretch', he joined the RNVR. For the first eight months he organized the desperately urgent business of repairing coastal craft. By 1944 he had become Director of Combined Operations Material.

In 1945 he became Chairman of the Commonwealth Telecommunications Conference, and from the next year until 1950 was Chairman of the Commonwealth Telecommunications Board, responsible for the re-ordering of all cable and wireless systems in the British Commonwealth, a job of the utmost complexity.

After that, there were many public appointments — and, from 1953, directorships in commerce. His autobiography, *Into the Wind*, was published in 1949 and, in 1960, *Wearing Spurs*. At the close of 1966 he had the great satisfaction of becoming Lord Rector of Glasgow University.

During his years in the BBC he had found time to write his highly entertaining reminiscence, *Wearing Spurs*. It was typical of the man that he hid it in a drawer lest it cause embarrassment to the great institution of which he was Director-General, and only published it in 1960, after yet another war had come and gone. Perhaps he was right; for the image of stern rectitude which the BBC had somehow built up between wars might have been confused by the reminiscences of a founder who clearly loved 'wearing spurs' — a man who would have made an unorthodox and highly successful general.

Sir Robert Watson-Watt

To many of us born between the two World Wars, the battle of Britain remains not only one of the fixed points in history, but an event surpassing in importance Waterloo, Thermopylae, and the invention of the steam engine.

Odd, in fact, that the outcome of the Battle of Britain should have been so influenced by a direct descendant of the developer of that steam engine, James Watt — usually credited with being its inventor — whose story is on another page. Robert Watson-Watt, like his ancestor James, was not exactly the inventor of radar, but he did more than any other single man to develop it, make it effective.

Did, in short, more than any other single man to win that Battle of Britain.

As he himself has listed it, success in that battle is owed, first to

208

the fighter pilots themselves whose courage and training outfought the Germans; second, to the Spitfire and Hurricane aircraft which gave them some small advantages over their opposite numbers in Messerschmitts; and thirdly to the effectiveness of what would some day be called radar.

Not that it was, at the time: by the time somebody thought up the word, the battle had been won.

Few of us, I imagine, who watched the vapour trails four and five miles above our heads in 1940 knew what part radar was playing in the battle we observed from down below, knew that a large number of that ragged-seeming German bomber formation had been intercepted and shot down over the English Channel, before entering English skies. We had little idea that the formation had been detected by some magic device which saw through mist and fog and darkness to pinpoint an enemy formation — or even a single aircraft — even before it had left the coast of France; and could direct the Spitfires on to it.

For that matter, hardly any of us knew that the aircraft alert at eleven a.m. on the Sunday, that Sunday, 3 September, of Mr Chamberlain's declaration of war, had been caused by the effective functioning of this new device. Captain de Brantes, the Assistant French Military Attaché, was returning by air from France and had omitted to tell anyone of his plan. Radio-location (to give it the name it enjoyed at the time) picked up this one small aeroplane as it left the French coast — and the rest is history. Fortunately for the gallant captain and for Anglo-French relations, his identity was revealed before a flight of Hurricanes dropped him in the Channel.

Before we look at the father of radio-location, let us examine the child.

Radio waves — short ones, long ones, and those in between, all travel at the speed of light — to which, of course, they are close cousins. In our own archaic units of measurement this speed is 186,000 miles a second. In more enlightened lands, and in our own laboratories, this is shown more conveniently as 300 million metres a second. Furthermore, the speed is constant, so that when a radio voice says, 'Here is the news' — we know that those words are flying through space at this very great speed; they are not slowing down as they travel, like a cricket ball, or a bullet. And therefore, if by some means we can measure the time it takes for the words to reach us, we can easily calculate just how far away the radio station is.

We can, too, by the simple expedient of turning our portable radio to face in different directions till we hear the News at its loudest, get a reasonably accurate idea of the direction the waves are coming from. This latter principle had been in use for many years before real radio-location put in an appearance. A ship, without getting involved in the computer-arithmetic of micro-seconds which would tell it how far it was steaming from a shore transmitting station, could still plot its own position on a chart by taking bearings on two or more such stations. Where the lines drawn along the appropriate bearings from, say, Cardiff and Bristol, crossed on the chart — that was the ship's position.

So we can see that the theory behind this distance-and-direction-finding by radio was not exactly new.

But this, of course, is not to belittle the remarkable experimental physicist who had the vision, the drive, and above all, the patience, to make something out of it. A part of the secret of radio-location's success lies in the personality of the man himself. Robert Watson-Watt knew he was right, knew he was going to make it work and work well. He also knew he would be able to make others see his point, and do something about developing his brain child.

In this major respect Watson-Watt differs from Baird. He had the Scots pugnacity to go with his imagination. Without the combination he might well never have succeeded in getting the all-out support of his government to make his brain-child grow — and earn its keep.

In the United States, men like Hoyt Taylor were working along much the same lines, but the US Government, on this occasion, made little effort to help them. Even despite the successes of British radio-location during the first two years of war, successes which were freely acknowledged by American observers, Pearl Harbour, on its fatal day, was equipped with out-of-date and inadequate equipment, which was manned by unskilled operators. These in turn were mistrusted by those to whom they passed on their reports. A flight of about a dozen American B17 bombers was expected in from San Francisco: when something like ten times this number of aircraft were shown as coming from the opposite direction no one believed it. And so Pearl Harbour nearly died.

Robert Watson-Watt was born 13 April, 1892, at Brechin in the County of Angus, down in that eastern corner north of the Tay, where so many of our famous people seem to have been born. His father was a carpenter and by hard work the boy got himself via Brechin High School to University College, Dundee, a part of the University of St Andrews. At the age of twenty, armed with his BSc, he was teaching physics at the same University College.

But shortly afterwards he was invited to join the Meteorological Office of the new Royal Aircraft Establishment at Farnborough: he accepted with some misgiving, though the prospects seemed good, for a study of wind and rain seemed at a far remove from the heavy engineering which had been his first love.

Fortunately for all of us, the job young Watson-Watt was given to do caught his imagination and, though he could hardly have spotted the similarity at first, was closely involved with the principles on which he would some day develop his radio-location. The Royal Aircraft Establishment wanted to be able to warn aircraft of thunderstorms, and to this end Watson-Watt began to experiment with atmospherics. As we all know, these are picked up by radio receivers and are at their worst during thunderstorms — for a flash of lightning is about the biggest atmospheric with which we have to deal.

The system of radio direction-finding, whereby, as we've seen, a ship can plot its position by taking bearings of two radio stations, can be adapted so that two receivers and aerials can take the bearings of a single radio station and plot its position. In the same way — at least in theory — the position of a flash of lightning could be found, however far away, or even out of sight.

There are obvious difficulties about this: lightning doesn't stay still, waiting to be measured. But now Robert Watson-Watt set about his strange new hobby of chasing these lightning flashes. It was a prospect that would have daunted most scientists because of the practical difficulties involved, but to Watson-Watt this was only a challenge to be met.

He thought about it — and wrote to the BBC. Would they let him have the text of a series of talks which were going to be given by Sir Walford Davies, Master of the King's Musick? They would be called 'Music and the Ordinary Listener'.

Obviously, you say, the man was mad.

But he was not. It *was* just this Ordinary Listener he wanted, and now Watson-Watt persuaded him — a whole army of him — to listen to the talks, script in hand. As he described it himself, each listener would mark on his copy of the script the 'syllables which were mutilated by atmospherics as he listened; the relative intensity of the atmospheric was indicated by the number of lines he drew through the syllable; the duration of the disturbance was recorded by making the lines begin and end on the syllables on which audible disturbances began and ended. Disturbances falling between words were indicated by crosses, of size roughly proportional to intensity, in the appropriate places.'

This strange team of co-opted scientists, all over Britain, listened for ten minutes on each of seven evenings during the summer of 1926. The information the team provided was so revealing that the net was then spread far wider, from North Africa to Norway, Ireland to Germany. The findings revealed that many of the atmospherics audible on ordinary broadcast receivers came from as far away as *4,500 miles*.

Not content with them, Watson-Watt embarked on a cruiser, HMS *Yarmouth*, to pursue his lightning flashes round the world as far as the Bay of Bengal. On his return he disembarked in Egypt and went with his wife to Cairo and Khartoum to take observations from both these points.

The scientific work went on, and many developments in weather forecasting as well as aerial navigation stem from it, but now, in the start of 1935, he got a strange request from the British Government.

Did Mr Watson-Watt have any ideas about a Death Ray?

Those of us who remember those 'tween-war years will remember that one of the many things which (like today's H-bomb) would 'make war impossible, unthinkable' was the 'Death Ray'. Oh, it was a terrible thing, the Death Ray; not only had it 'in secret trials' killed people at great distances (apparently they were condemned murderers who were given this splendid chance of serving king and country), but the Rays would ground the whole of an enemy air force, paralyse an army's transport by short-circuiting ignition systems. As for the enemy's ammunition, if he still had the heart to want to use any after all these distressing setbacks, that could be exploded by Death Rays long before he got round to loading it up.

The only trouble with the Death Ray was that it did not exist. And now Robert Watson-Watt pointed out that it almost certainly never would.

Then, as an afterthought, he wrote in his report to the government that there was a good chance of using a 'ray' to spot the position of enemy aircraft, a form of 'radio-location', seeing through cloud or darkness. He added this rider merely in order to relieve some of the gloom of his report; the government had wanted its Death Ray; he could not produce one, but as a sop he offered a Detection Ray.

The result was a government request for enlightenment, preferably by demonstration. And this, at remarkably short notice, Watson-Watt arranged.

There are, at this very moment, many short-wave radio transmitters in Britain, beaming programmes in many languages to many parts of the world. In 1935 there were fewer of them, but Watson-Watt decided to make use of one which transmitted a powerful signal on fifty metres.

He would work on the known fact that, as we have seen, the distance and direction of a radio transmitter can be fairly easily calculated. An enemy aircraft was not a radio transmitter, but if it could be persuaded to *reflect* the wave from that transmitter back to earth again, the same process could be adapted to discover its position in the air.

But would an aeroplane reflect a sufficiently powerful signal? Would the reflected signal be strong enough to detect, analyse?

It was — and at Daventry in the English midlands, in February, 1935, radio-location was born. Eight miles away the aircraft reflected sufficient of the Daventry short-wave station's signal to the home-made apparatus on the ground, for a clear indication to be shown on the visual indicator. When the old Heyford passed overhead, the little stub of vertical line on the screen grew to its maximum. Then it shrank, till at eight and a quarter miles it vanished.

At this point in his career, Watson-Watt was superintendent of the new Radio Division at the National Physical Laboratory in Teddington. He now left this important job in order to follow up the exciting new idea of radio-location — and many people thought he was throwing away his career in pursuit of a will-o'-the-wisp. But he was to write later that he was absolutely certain he and his team would succeed and he 'never doubted for a moment that everything would work out, with many delays and a few blind alleys, to an effective warning system. I believe, too, that our predominant feeling was a lively anticipation of privileged fun in playing such a fascinating game to win which was certain, although the final score could not be estimated.'

The team set up its HQ on a remote part of the Suffolk coast, near Orfordness. The work had to be kept secret and all sorts of cloaks were patched together to explain what all these young men were doing with their instruments and their masts; they were making a 'death ray'; they were prospecting for oil; doing a dozen other improbable things. A few service personnel now joined them, but these, of course, worked in civilian clothes.

A few months after starting at Orford the team moved a mile or so away to the stately Manor of Bawdsey, to complete the work in greater secrecy. By this time, held together by the forceful and brilliant Scot, it had solved many of the problems of radio-location. The time taken for a radio wave (not one borrowed from the BBC as before, but sent out by their own miniature transmitter) to travel to an aircraft and be reflected back again was represented visually on the face of a cathode-ray tube (the screen, in fact, of a television receiver) and the length of the fluorescent green line on the face showed the distance involved. The transmitter directed its radio signal along a narrow beam — not broadcast like a normal radio transmitter, which deliberately splashes programmes in all directions more or less indiscriminately — and it was a fairly simple matter to note in which direction the movable transmitting aerial was pointing and from this to see in which direction the aircraft would be found. The altering length of the fluorescent line, the changed direction of the aerial, and the rate at which these changes took place, showed which direction the aircraft was travelling, and at what speed.

By December of this year, 1935, the system was so advanced that it was decided to set up five radio-location stations on the east coast. By March of the following year, aircraft were being plotted at distances of up to seventy-five miles. The signals were sent out from masts 240 feet in the air, and these same masts, some millionths of a second later, received their reflection.

During 1936 the training of RAF personnel to man these stations began, and plans were laid for another twenty stations. As the process was refined, new developments became possible: Ground-Controlled Interception could direct defending aircrtaft right up to an approaching enemy; searchlights could be directed on to enemy aircraft before the light beam was switched on, and then be automatically locked to that aircraft so that it was unable to escape from the beam; aircraft themselves could carry equipment which would locate enemy warships; and so on.

In 1937, with the threat of war growing imminent, Watson-Watt and his wife were sent as tourists to Germany to investigate what progress, if any, the Germans had made along the same lines. They plodded from place to place, made sketches, took photographs, fooled everyone — and for this act of bravery they deserve our heartfelt gratitude. They reported that the Germans seemed to have very little in the way of radio-locating equipment — and the war, when it came two years later, proved this correct.

1938. And now, with Watson-Watt working directly for the Air Ministry, there was twenty-four-hour-a-day radio-location cover of the North Sea approaches. No plane was able to approach Britain from the east without being tracked. And yet the system was still top secret and hardly anyone — least of all the Germans — knew of it.

War came — and now we may abandon the cumbersome but accurate name under which it was developed, and adopt the

American 'radar', that sensible shortening of 'radio detection and ranging'. There had been considerable American work on a similar system, and when the Battle of Britain proved beyond all doubt the effectiveness of Watson-Watt's brainchild, American teams were sent over to study it. British scientists began to make regular visits to the United States to co-ordinate development.

With the Battle of Britain a disastrous German failure, the Luftwaffe took to night bombing. It is an indication of the development and expansion of radar that whereas in the whole of December, 1940, RAF night fighters shot down only two German bombers, they destroyed, in May, 1941, over a hundred.

The research establishment now moved from Bawdsey to Swanage — where it was attacked by a desperate Luftwaffe. It went on, shaken but functioning, to Malvern College, where it stayed till the end of the war (while Malvern, as a school, moved to Harrow; the happy combination, to those inside, was simply 'Marrow'). To the great mass of the British public its work was a baffling secret, and when Watson-Watt was given a knighthood in 1942 the citation only hinted at the service he had rendered his country.

The war ended and Sir Robert Watson-Watt stayed on as a government scientific adviser until 1949. By this time radar had become an indispensable adjunct of civil air navigation, blind landing for aircraft and their maritime equivalent, getting ships into port in a fog. Douglas in the Isle of Man was the first harbour in the world to be equipped with radar apparatus giving a complete picture of the approaches through any fog. Since then many other ports have followed suit.

Work on applications of the radar principle are still going on, and possibly always will, with the development of new, miniature components, new materials, new ideas. Navigational radar, directing aircraft over hundreds of miles to within a few yards of a target, was brought to a high pitch of development during the war, making possible 1,000-bomber raids on places like Cologne. Possibilities are limitless. It could be made impossible for aircraft to collide in the air or crash into hillsides (or for cars to crash into each other). It has already been found possible to land an aircraft in zero visibility without a pilot at all, and the pilotless aircraft is no longer a silly story ('Please fasten your seat-belts, your seat-belts, your seat-belts, your seat-belts — '), but a definite probability for the future.

An exciting new development is radio-astronomy, based on exactly the same principles. Scientists tried aiming radar at the moon to check its distance and its relative movement, and were surprised at getting back a great deal more, radiowise, than they had given; there were literally hundreds of different signals coming from outer space. It was shown that these came from stars, many of them too far away to be seen by eye or telescope: from this discovery sprang the whole new field of radio-astronomy which not only reveals great unknown regions, but is just as effective by daylight as by night.

Sir Robert Watson-Watt has been described — by some people — as a 'difficult' man, ready to burst into print on almost any subject and rightly jealous of the part he played in the development of this amazing new branch of science. There was heated controversy after the war about whether the developer of radar and his team should receive some financial recognition of their work which had been handed over gratis to both the British and American governments. After considerable acrimony, and argument as to exactly who had invented radar, a sum of £87,950 was awarded (the sort of sum that only a British government could conceive, and one wonders why they omitted the odd shillings). The team had already agreed on the size of each man's share: Sir Robert got £52,000.

Not perhaps a very large sum, for saving his country.

Appendix

Places to visit and things to do

Fascinating as it has been to write about the lives and achievements of these men and women, the tracking down of things and places has been in some cases disappointing, even disillusioning. The Scottish Tourist Board, 23 Ravelston Terrace, Edinburgh EH4 3EU and my own Aberdeen Central Library have both been hard at work on my behalf and I am most grateful to both of them. But a number of famous folk have managed to kick over the traces, so that little remains. Societies honouring the memory of people like Sir Harry Lauder change Secretaries (and leave no forwarding address). Mary Garden, through being economical with the truth about her year of birth, now has a splendid plaque in the place where she wasn't born. And so on.

But I have set out what I know of places and things in Scotland which may be of interest to readers. As these short biographies are all of men and women who had their greatest success outside Scotland, some entries are very short indeed. The real wonder of Carnegie's achievement is in the United States, as are those of Alexander Graham Bell. Lord Reith's monument is Broadcasting House in London; and two of our great men lie in Westminster Abbey.

No doubt there are more details available than those I have listed. Local Tourist Boards and Councils are usually eager to show them.

1)   Robert Adam, most famous of the brothers, was born 1728 in Kirkcaldy overlooking the firth of Forth. Many of the buildings and whole districts we owe to his genius, in Scotland and England, are described in his biography. He is buried in Westminster Abbey.

2)   James Watt was born 1736 in Greenock on the Clyde, near

Glasgow. I know of no memorial to him there, but in Chambers Street, Edinburgh, there is a statue outside the Heriot-Watt Building. And almost every bit of electrical equipment you buy will show his name, from the humble 40-Watt light bulb, via the telly and the video, to the umpteen-thousand-Watt electric cooker.

3) James Boswell was born 1740 and is more fortunate, having a fine museum at the old family home in Auchinleck, Ayrshire. The Cumnock & Doon Valley Tourist Association (see Keir Hardie entry) and the Auchinleck Boswell Society, 131 Main Street, Auchinleck, Ayr, are both very helpful. The museum was once the parish church, dating from 900 A.D., with, somewhat later, the Boswell family mausoleum next door.

4) John McAdam was born 1756 in Ayr. As a tenth son he was sent to New York, aged fourteen, to stay with his uncle. He returned, a married man, in 1783 to purchase the Ayrshire estate of Sauchrie.

5) Thomas Telford was born 1757, 'near' Langholm, Dumfries-shire, in what would have been little more than a mud hut, and was orphaned a few months later. He was a successful and talented apprentice mason to Andrew Thomson in Langholm and his mark is still on the bridge there, along with other works, including his own father's gravestone with its wonderful inscription. He left behind him thousands of miles of road, also churches, bridges, harbours and canals, of which the Caledonian Canal, joining east coast to west, is the most famous in Scotland. The Dean Bridge, five minutes from Princes Street in Edinburgh, is a fine example of his work.

6) George Gordon Byron was born 1788 in lodgings off London's Cavendish Square, but almost immediately his Scots mother — deserted by his English father, 'Mad Jack' Byron — took him to Aberdeen, where they lived at 68 Broad Street. Between the ages of six and ten he attended the Aberdeen Grammar School in School-hill. This has now been demolished and replaced by a fine complex

in Skene Street, graced in the forecourt by a statue of Byron. There is a Grammar School story that when Byron succeeded to the peerage on the death of a great-uncle, and his name was read out at roll call as 'Georgi Domine de Byron', he burst into tears and fled from the room. At the age of eight, convalescing from scarlet fever, he spent a summer at Ballatrech Farmhouse near Ballater. It had a lasting effect on him and he often referred to it in his work. The farmhouse is now largely rebuilt. Byron left Scotland for ever aged ten, but maintained throughout that he was 'a whole Scot'.

7)   David Livingstone was born 1813 in Blantyre on the Clyde, eight miles from Glasgow. The David Livingstone Memorial is there, with the room in which he was born, and a fine display combining Africa and the Industrial Revolution. He is buried in Westminster Abbey.

8)   Andrew Carnegie was born 1835 in a weaver's cottage in Moodie Street, Dunfermline. It remains, and in 1928 his widow opened the Memorial Hall adjoining. It symbolises the poles of this extraordinary man's career. Almost opposite is the entrance to Pittencrieff Park, Carnegie's gift to his native town. Gifts to Dunfermline give an idea of the scope of his generosity in countless other places: The Carnegie Free Baths, 1877; Carnegie Free Library, 1883; Technical School, 1889; New Carnegie Baths, 1905; Pittencrieff Park and Glen, 1903. His benefactions remain all over the United States. He is buried in the Sleepy Hollow Cemetery, Lennox, Mass.

9)   Alexander Graham Bell was born 1847 in South Charlotte Street, Edinburgh. There is a memorial plaque at Number Sixteen.

10)   Mary Slessor was born 1848 in the now vanished street of Mutton Brae, Aberdeen. She was christened at the United Presbyterian Church in nearby Belmont Street, and there is a memorial plaque. From the age of eleven until her departure for Africa she and her family lived in Dundee.

11)   Robert Louis Stevenson was born 1850 at 8 Howard Place, Edinburgh, but lived much of his early life in his father's house at 17 Heriot Row (which can be visited). The Tourist authorities have devised a 'Stevenson Trail' starting at Lady Stair's House in the High Street, which has a museum; it goes on to Heriot Row; then to the wooded hamlet of Swanton which R.L.S. so loved; then South Queensferry and its Hawes Inn, which he was fond of visiting. There is an effigy of him in Edinburgh's Wax Museum. Near North Berwick is the Island of Fidra, which can be visited. This is mentioned in 'Catriona' and may well have been 'Treasure Island'.

12)   Keir Hardie was born 1856 in the tiny village of Legbrannoch near Holytown in Lanarkshire. He lived much of his life in Cumnock, Ayrshire, where he edited the 'Cumnock News' and where the house he built, 'Lochnorris' in Auchinleck Road, still stands. Information about Hardie — and James Boswell — can be obtained from the Cumnock & Doon Valley Tourist Association, 1 New Street, Dalmellington, Ayr.

13)   James Barrie was born 1860 in what I have earlier described as 'an absurdly small cottage'. In fact, Number Nine Brechin Road, Kirriemuir would have been a very adequate dwelling for a normal family, but not for David and Margaret's eight children. (Two others had died in infancy.) It is now a Barrie museum with original manuscripts and various mementoes. Kirriemuir is the 'Thrums' of his novels. The famous Peter Pan statue is in Kensington Gardens, London.

14)   Ramsay Macdonald was born 1866 in a two-roomed cottage in Lossiemouth, near Inverness. He was a pupil and subsequently, for two years, a teacher at the village school in nearby Drainie. He died 1937 at sea and his body was brought back to be buried beside that of his wife in Lossiemouth.

15)   Sir Harry Lauder was born 1870 at Portobello on the coast near Edinburgh. There is a plaque in his honour at Number Three

Bridge Street. But it is at Hamilton, near Glasgow, where he died, that a section of the Hamilton Museum has been devoted to his life. At the time of writing, the Secretary of the Harry Lauder Society is a very helpful lady residing at 1 Cammo Gardens, Edinburgh EH4 8EJ.

16)   Mary Garden's birth certificate, which I have seen, reveals that she was born 1874 at 35 Charlotte Street, Aberdeen. But as she always insisted she was born 1877, and we know that her parents moved to 41 Dee Street in 1875, it has been (I suppose) a pretty gesture to site her birth plaque there. Chicopee, Massachusetts, deserves the credit for 'discovering' her.

17)   John Buchan, 1st Baron Tweedsmuir, was born 1875 in the manse of the Knox Church, Perth.

18)   Sir Alexander Fleming was born 1881 at Loundon in Ayrshire. There is a plaque outside the window in St Mary's Hospital, Paddington, London, where he discovered penicillin.

19)   John Logie Baird was born 1888 in Helensburgh on the Clyde, where there is a bust on display.

20)   John Reith, 1st Baron of Stonehaven, was born 1889 in the manse at Evan Street, Stonehaven, on the coast south of Aberdeen.

21)   Sir Robert Watson-Watt was born 1892 in Brechin, where he attended the High School.

Index